HIGH MAGIK 303
David Thompson

HIGH MAGIK 303

David Thompson

✷ Trans Mundane ✷
Publishing
—— Occult Knowledge ——

Copyright © 2025 David Thompson

All rights reserved.

ISBN-13: 978-1-961765-48-1

No part of this book may be reproduced in any form, electronic or other, without express written permission from the author and publisher. Please respect the author's copyright.

Cover: David Thompson

To Lilith

A Thaum is the basic unit of magical strength. It has been universally established as the amount of magic needed to create one small white pigeon or three normal-sized billiard balls.

-Terry Pratchett

A Legal Disclaimer:

By Law, I am obliged to let you know that this is for entertainment purposes only, and does not claim to prevent or cure any diseases. The advice in this book should not be construed as financial, medical, or psychological advice. Please seek such advice from a professional.

By purchasing this book, and working the rituals, you understand that results are not guaranteed. In light of this and in the unlikely event that the material in this book does not work for you or, in the very unlikely event, this book causes physical harm to you or a loved one, you agree that you will not hold David Thompson, our affiliates and employees liable for any damages you may experience or incur.

Each individual's success depends on his or her background, dedication, desire, and motivation.

All material is Copyright © 2025 David Thompson, All Rights Reserved.

A Warning:

This is very powerful material. When worked properly, you may see unexpected results. These rituals and petitions are like electricity, the energy will flow in the direction of the intended output. In saying this, please be firm in your intentions and make absolutely sure what you want is truly want you desire.

As they say, be careful what you wish for, you just might get it.

Introduction 1
   My Magik System 2
   Becoming a Master of Your Own Magik 3
CHAPTER 1 5
   Developing Your Own Rituals 5
CHAPTER 2 12
   Ye Olde Tyme Rituals 12
CHAPTER 3 18
   Creating Your Personal Magik System 18
   The Four Core Elements of a Personal Magik System 22
CHAPTER 4 25
   The Role of Meditation in Magik 25
   Astral Travel: Unlocking the Gateway to Unlimited Power 31
   Building Your Astral Temple 35
   Working a Ritual in the Astral 39
   Astral Weapons & Defense: Creating Tools for Protection in Non-Physical Realms 41
CHAPTER 5 49
   Time & Reality Manipulation 49
   Jumping Timelines—How to Shift to a Better Version of Your Reality 56
   The Observer Effect 68
CHAPTER 6 71
   Developing Pathworking 71
CHAPTER 7 80
   A Personal Grimoire 80
   Living Grimoire 87
CHAPTER 8 90
   Magikal Experimentation & Psychic Development 90
   Using the Pendulum & Tarot 98
   Detecting Energy Currents 100
CHAPTER 9 104
   Engineering Reality 104
   Becoming The Creator 107
   Limitless Manifestation 112
CHAPTER 10 117

    Contacting Any Spirit 117
    Researching Spirits 123
    Preparing for Contact 128
    Ritual for Spirit Communication 132
    Troubleshooting 139
CHAPTER 11 143
    Difficult Magik 143
    Fast Money Magik – Why It "Doesn't Work" 148
    Love Magik - the "Most Difficult" 152
    Immortality 155
    Defying Reality 159
    Making the Impossible Possible 162
CHAPTER 12 165
    Oils and Powders 165
    The Power in Magik Powders 169
    Recipes 172
Glossary of Terms 177
About The Author 185

Introduction

This is *High Magik 303*, a sequel to *High Magik 101*.

Don't go hunting for *High Magik 202*—I skipped that and went straight to *High Magik 303*.

You see, when I was in college (University of Texas/Austin), most classes were structured as 301, 302, 303, etc., with 301 indicating a beginner's class. Three credit hours, three hours a week.

Thus, High Magik 303. The first book should have been called High Magik 301, but then people would've been wondering where High Magik 101 and 202 were.

So.

Welcome to High Magik 303!

This book is slightly more advanced than High Magik 101.

Here, we'll cover advanced practices that don't rely on any one specific spirit. Topics include making initial contact with unknown spirits, researching specific spirits, crafting rituals, communicating with spirits, getting pathworking steps from spirits, pacts, and more.

A lot of this book focuses on *non-ritual magik*—pathworking, astral travel, and other direct applications. But don't worry, astral is surprisingly easy once you learn a single trick. And yes, I'll teach you that trick in this book.

I will also talk about meditation. Now, I'm one of those people who reject most traditional meditation practices. I don't see much point in them beyond training the mind to focus and remain calm. But when you inject visualization into meditation, you get something that actually works for magik. Yes, sitting in meditation can calm the mind, but forcing people to meditate as a required part of magik? Not necessary.

Towards the end, I'll explore what I call Difficult Magik, which includes sex magik and fortune magik.

Why "Difficult?"

Two reasons. First, fortune magik—our beliefs often limit what we can actually achieve with it. Second, love/sex magik—because we're dealing with another person, and it's never a guaranteed outcome. You can't really make someone jump into bed with you or elope to Vegas to be married by a circus clown/mime in an Elvis costume. (Though, if you do pull that off, I want the full story.)

My Magik System

If you've read my other books, you can probably skip this

section. But for those new to my work, let's talk about my magik system.

First, the term High Magik wasn't mine. I just called what I was doing magik, but others started calling it High Magik.

According to some random A.I. chatbot I asked, High Magik is defined as:

"High magick, also known as ceremonial magic or ritual magic, is a diverse set of rituals and practices that involve ceremony and accessories."

It usually involves summoning or invoking spirits—whether deities or daemons. Some people equate it with Wicca and Witchcraft, but while there are similarities, they're fundamentally different.

Now, my system?

I throw most of that out the window.

I also play fast and loose with definitions.

Such as Manifestation or Magick? Same thing. For me, "summoning" and "invocation" mean the same thing.

One absolute rule: Light the candles, THEN turn off the room lights.

Becoming a Master of Your Own Magik

It's time for you to become the master of your own magik.

- Move beyond structured High Magik into personalized mastery.
- Develop your own rituals instead of relying on traditional systems.

- Break free from rigid structures—craft your own powerful magik.
- Master the three pillars of advanced magik:
- Personal Rituals, Astral Mastery, and Reality Manipulation.

Final Notes

This is your journey. Your magik. Your power.

High Magik 303 isn't about memorizing someone else's system—it's about building your own.

Let's begin.

CHAPTER 1

Developing Your Own Rituals

To develop your own rituals, you can start with mine as a template. My rituals are stripped down, straightforward, and designed to be as simple as possible while still holding power. They aren't cluttered with unnecessary steps or excess theatrics. They work because they contain only what's needed.

But the real truth? A ritual isn't always necessary. A skilled magician can work magik without one—anytime, anywhere. I do it all the time. Most experienced magicians do. Magik is intention, force, and precision—the ritual is just a structure that helps channel that power.

Still, there's value in using rituals, especially when you're developing your own system. Rituals create consistency and teach you how to direct power in a way that's repeatable. That's where we start—not by blindly following pre-written rituals, but by understanding how they work. That way, when you create your own, they aren't just random actions thrown together—they're deliberate constructions of power.

Learning The Rules (Before Breaking Them)

Since I was a teenager, this has been my approach to everything—photography, writing, filmmaking. I learned the rules first—not so I could follow them forever, but so I could break them properly.

If you don't know the mechanics of something, breaking it is just guesswork. But if you understand why something works the way it does, then when you break it, you're refining it. That's a huge difference.

Magik is no different.

Some people hear about personal ritual and think it means making things up on the fly. It doesn't. There's a difference between personal magik and random trial and error. Too many people toss out structured magik because they think rules limit them. The truth is, rules exist because they work.

The difference between a structured ritual and a personal ritual is simple:

- Structured rituals are designed for general use.
- Personal rituals are tailored specifically to you.
- But the underlying principles—the real rules—don't

High Magik 303

change.
- Structured rituals have been around for centuries for a reason. They're based on energetic laws that don't suddenly stop working just because modern magicians want to take shortcuts.
- Casting a circle isn't just some ceremonial tradition—it creates a defined space, shifts perception, and establishes a controlled environment for energy to move.
- Lighting a candle isn't just symbolic—it anchors fire energy into the ritual, directing the force of transformation and creation.
- Invoking a spirit or deity isn't about memorizing poetic words—it's about creating a connection between your energy and a greater force.

When you work with structured rituals, ask yourself:
- What is each step actually accomplishing?
- Is it necessary, or is it just ritualistic excess?
- What energies or forces does this ritual align with?
- If you remove or replace something, does it weaken the ritual or strengthen it?

Magik isn't about copying ancient words or gathering a collection of expensive props. It's about moving energy, aligning power, and shaping reality with precision. If a ritual's structure helps with that, keep it. If something feels forced, unnecessary, or just doesn't generate power, strip it away.

Breaking structure isn't about throwing things out—it's about removing what isn't working and reinforcing what is.

Experiment and Observe

Magik is not theoretical. It's not something you read about and assume will work just because it's in a book. It has to be tested, adjusted, and experienced directly.

This is where many people fail.

- Some follow structured rituals word-for-word, assuming they must be perfect as written.
- Others rush into personal ritual too soon, without ever proving whether their methods are effective.

Both approaches lead to weak magik.

Magik isn't just about performing rituals. It's about working them—pushing against them, watching how they respond, and refining them in real time.

The only way to know if a ritual works for you is to run it exactly as written and observe. That gives you a baseline—a control sample. You're not just casting a spell; you're measuring its effect.

Ask yourself:
- Does the energy build naturally?
- Does it flow smoothly?
- Does the structure help you stay focused, or does it feel restrictive?
- Does the ritual feel powerful or mechanical?
- Do you sense real movement of energy, or is it just a

series of actions?

Some rituals have been passed down because they consistently work. Others have stuck around purely out of tradition, not effectiveness. You won't know which is which until you experience them firsthand.

Once you've worked a structured ritual, then you start breaking it apart. Strip it down, swap elements, replace tools with something that aligns better with your energy.

If a structured ritual feels ineffective, something is missing.

- Maybe the wording lacks force.
- Maybe the method is outdated.
- Maybe the entire structure doesn't align with how you channel energy.
- If your adjustments strengthen the ritual, you're moving in the right direction. If they weaken it, step back.

Change one piece at a time and watch the effect. If a personal ritual feels scattered or unstable, something is off. Some rituals collapse under their own looseness. If the power dissipates too fast, it needs structure to hold it together.

This is the key to balancing fluidity and structure.

- A ritual that's too rigid blocks the natural flow of energy.
- A ritual that's too open scatters power before it can take effect.

Magik should be fluid, but never vague. The balance is

found through direct experience.

The Path to Mastery: Intuition, Tracking, and Owning Your Magik

Magik is a force. You don't just use it—you become it.

The most powerful rituals don't come from blindly following traditions. They come from direct experience—from rituals that have been tested, adjusted, stripped down, and rebuilt until they generate the strongest results possible.

Your subconscious already knows what works. It picks up on resonance and emptiness.

If a word, a tool, a movement, or a step in a ritual feels unnatural, it isn't for you.

Magik responds to confidence, not hesitation.

If something doesn't align with your personal current, discard it.

But instinct alone isn't enough.

A magician who doesn't track their work is just guessing.

Magik is refined through experience, not memory.

What worked? What didn't?

What unexpectedly shifted reality?

What felt powerful in the moment but faded fast?

What small change created a massive shift?

Personal ritual is a process, not a final product.

A magician who doesn't keep a record of their work repeats the same mistakes. But a magician who tracks every detail, tests every adjustment, and refines their process?

High Magik 303

That's someone who moves beyond practicing magik into owning it.

At some point, every magician has to stop being a student of magik and become the source of it.

Personal ritual isn't just about rewriting spells—it's a declaration that you no longer need someone else's system to access power.

You move beyond following.

You become the system.

That's the difference between a practitioner and a master.

CHAPTER 2

Ye Olde Tyme Rituals

I had an English teacher who loved assigning "compare and contrast" essays. The entire class would groan, then buckle down to read and write.

Groaning aside, that's exactly what I'm going to do here.

I'm pulling an old magik book and paraphrasing one of its rituals, then I'll contrast it with how I'd rewrite that same ritual. Due to copyright issues, I won't list the book's title, but readers familiar with it will recognize the ritual I've chosen.

It's not just the ritual itself that's archaic—it's the preparation and steps leading up to it. This is like diving into an ancient grimoire, packed with references to celestial timings, guardians (usually the four archangels), evocations

High Magik 303

meant to bind the summoned spirit, and safeguards in case the spirit was so evil that it might steal the magician's soul, dooming them to eternal damnation.

Damn. Seriously? Anyway.

Breaking Down the Archaic Ritual

I'll start by looking at the original ritual.

The ritual in this text calls upon an obscure genius spirit—a tricky and slippery entity, so one had to take extra precautions.

- First, carefully draw a protection sigil by hand.
- Bless the drawing with special incense smoke.
- Wear the sigil along with a specially crafted fabric tunic.
- Hold a specially crafted wand.

But that's just the beginning.

Before even attempting the ritual, one had to fast—no food or drink for a full day—followed by a cleansing bath with salt and various oils. (Basically, a magikal day spa.)

On the appointed day and time, the magician would:
- Go to their altar.
- Ensure a special symbol was hung on the north wall.
- Lay out a blessed length of twine in a circle to define their sacred space.
- Stand on one leg while meditating and repeating a

special phrase like a mantra—for at least five minutes.
- Call on the guardians by repeating prayers and psalms while facing each direction.
- Hold one hand high while pointing at the ground with the wand. (Oops, forgot that step? Start over.)

Now, after wobbling on one leg, repeating mantras, and adjusting hand placements, it's time to light the candles.

And incense.

BUT FIRST
- The altar must be laid out in a specific pattern for this spirit.
- Four additional symbols must be placed at each corner of the altar.
- Only after chanting can anything else continue.
- In the dark, until you light the candles.

Then light the incense. Not just any incense—a rare blend with ingredients that are impossible to find today.

Now, it's finally time to evoke the spirit—using a binding spell to drag the spirit from the "depths of hell" into the circle.

(If this were a satire, this would be the part where the spirit steps into the circle fresh out of the bath, wrapped in a towel, with curlers in their hair. But no, we're serious here.)

Next, the magician demands the spirit move on their behalf, binding them in the circle until the wish is granted. If the spirit refuses, they are condemned to eternity in hell—where they already reside.

If everything works? The magik might manifest in about three months.

Maybe.

Simplifying the Ritual

Now, let's be practical.

After reading an archaic ritual like this, I break it down into basic steps, research the spirit, and determine what's actually needed. Then, instead of commanding and binding the spirit, I ask politely.

I treat spirits with respect, whether I'm working for myself or for a paying client.

The goal is direct contact—without all the excessive steps—so the focus stays on manifesting the desire, not the theatrics.

Looking at each step of the old ritual, I'd say about 1% of it is necessary. The other 99% gets tossed.

Of course, some will argue that I must be protected from this evil spirit from the depths of hell. But that assumes:

1. The spirit actually resides in a place called "Hell."
2. The spirit is inherently evil.

The reality? Most non-physical spirits exist in the astral plane—often in a higher non-physical dimension.

Yes, there are nasty spirits—parasitic entities that feed off fear, anger, and chaos. Some magicians work with these entities because they thrive on drama and believe "Darkness" is the only path. In doing so, they become enslaved—feeding the spirit instead of the other way around.

The key to avoiding truly negative spirits is by increasing the frequency your own energy (ascending). By shifting our vibration higher, we naturally attract higher-vibrational spirits.

So.

Let's contrast my method with the archaic one:

My Streamlined Approach

- Create a sigil for the desire (mine or my client's).
- Make psychic contact with the spirit and ask what they actually want in terms of ritual.
  - Usually, it's just incense and a candle.
  - Some spirits are traditionalists and prefer blood offerings, but most are happy with red wine or another symbolic offering.
- Craft an invocation—usually a simple demonic ENN or a short summoning phrase.
- Drop all of this into my standard ritual—refined over decades of magik work.

I only cast a circle to create a portal, which helps slightly higher vibrational spirits step into our reality.

1. Candles? Set the atmosphere and anchor the energy.
2. Incense? Cleanses the space and clears lower vibrations.
3. Energize the candle with the intention to manifest the desire.
4. Give the offering.

Done.

That's it.

The Secret Sauce

What makes magik work?

Your intent. Your belief. Your certainty that it works.

Everything else? Just for show.

Maybe complex rituals trigger a response in those accustomed to religious traditions—it makes the process feel real. But at the end of the day, the elaborate steps aren't necessary.

Neither are astrological timings—unless you personally believe in them.

Magik isn't about overcomplicating the process.

If you feel drawn to intricate, ceremonial rituals, by all means—use them. But don't think that complexity equals power.

True mastery comes from understanding the core mechanics of magik and refining them into a process that works consistently.

That's the difference between following a system and becoming the system.

CHAPTER 3

Creating Your Personal Magik System

Magik isn't a museum exhibit. It's not something to be preserved in a glass case, untouched, with the expectation that it must always look and function exactly as it did centuries ago. Yet, plenty of practitioners cling to traditions like they're sacred law, as if deviating from them would cause the whole system to collapse.

They'll tell you that you need exact phrasing, specific tools, and perfect planetary alignments—that if you don't follow every step exactly as written, your magik won't work. But that mindset doesn't make magik stronger. It makes it stagnant.

The truth is, magik is adaptable. It evolves with the

practitioner, shaped by experience, necessity, and direct interaction with the forces being called. Rigid traditions fail to account for this. They set rules that might have made sense at the time they were created but don't necessarily apply to every magician, in every era, under every circumstance.

Spirits don't need a formal script to recognize a call. They don't care whether a ritual is performed in a dimly lit temple or an apartment bedroom—as long as the energy and intent are there.

The problem with rigid systems is that they trap the magician in repetition. You follow steps because that's what you were taught, not because you understand why those steps matter.

And that's where magik weakens.

You become dependent on external structure instead of developing personal authority. You second-guess your ability to alter a ritual because some long-dead author or self-proclaimed expert said it must be done a certain way. That kind of thinking kills creativity. It disconnects the magician from intuition and power.

Magik is personal. It responds to the individual, not the tradition.

A system should enhance a magician's ability—not restrict it. There's a difference between understanding the core principles of magik and blindly following a framework someone else built.

The strongest practitioners aren't the ones who memorize

the most rituals. They're the ones who learn how to shift and shape magik to fit their own will.

Experimentation Leads to Mastery

Real magik isn't about copying old instructions—it's about experimenting and testing different methods, adapting techniques, discarding what doesn't work, and refining what does.

This is how magik grows.

Spirits recognize power, not protocol. They appear because they are called with force, not because you read their names from the right book or lit the right candle.

Traditions are useful as a foundation, but they should never be a cage. Magik is alive, and the only way to fully tap into its potential is to treat it as something dynamic—something that bends and reshapes with practice.

The magician's role isn't to preserve the past. It's to work in the present—to wield magik as a force that moves with them, not against them.

That means breaking rules when necessary, discarding limits that serve no real purpose, and crafting a system that serves you, not the other way around.

Blending Different Magikal Influences into Something Uniquely Yours

Magik was never meant to be locked into a single system. It has always been an evolving force, shaped by those who practice it. Every culture, tradition, and method that exists today was once an innovation—someone's way of working with energy, refining techniques, adapting to what actually brought results.

The strongest magicians aren't those who chain themselves to a single path. They're the ones who recognize that magik is limitless—capable of being shaped and molded in ways that best serve the individual.

Blending different magikal influences isn't about throwing random elements together and hoping for the best. It's about understanding what works and why, then combining those elements into something functional and personal.

- Why do certain spirits respond to specific offerings?
- Why do certain ritual structures amplify results?
- Why do some methods shift energy more effectively than others?

When you understand those fundamentals, you're free to mix and adapt, to take what is useful from multiple traditions and discard what isn't.

There's a misconception that blending systems weakens them—that traditions must be kept pure to retain their power. But magik has never been pure.

Ancient magicians borrowed from each other constantly:

- The Greeks took from the Egyptians.
- The Romans took from the Greeks.
- Medieval grimoires pulled from every available source.

Magik has always been fluid, changing with time, place,

and the will of those practicing it.

The difference between an effective magician and one who struggles isn't the system they use.

It's their ability to take control of that system and make it their own.

The Four Core Elements of a Personal Magik System

To create a system that is truly yours, you need to consider four core elements:

1. Your Ritual Style—Structured, Freeform, or Channeled?

- Magik flows differently for every practitioner. Understanding your natural style strengthens your magik.
- Structured Magicians thrive on precision.
- Freeform Magicians shape their magik in the moment.
- Channeled Magicians receive direct guidance from spirits.

None of these approaches is superior. What matters is knowing what aligns with you best.

2. Your Personal Pantheon—Gods, Spirits, Egregores, or Pure Energy?

- Gods offer structured relationships and archetypal power.

- Spirits are direct, immediate, and highly interactive.
- Egregores are collective thought-forms, created by human belief.
- Pure energy-based magik bypasses entities entirely and works solely through force and intent.

The important thing is to know where your power comes from and how to interact with it effectively.

3. Your Core Symbols & Tools—Do You Need Them, or Can You Go Beyond?

Symbols act as shortcuts for the subconscious—they trigger deep responses and amplify intent.

Tools (candles, wands, altars) reinforce focus but are not required for magik to work.

The strongest magicians can generate the same results with or without physical objects.

4. Your Magikal Mindset—Belief Structures That Amplify Power

- Doubt weakens magik.
- Confidence strengthens it.
- Power follows expectation.

The most effective magicians command results. They don't ask—they make it happen.

Final Thoughts: Becoming the System

Some practitioners think they must commit to a single

system.

That magik only works if it's done one way, with one set of rules.

That's not how power functions.

Power is adaptable.

It moves through whatever conduit is available.

The magician's job isn't to follow the rules of a system—it's to make the system follow their will.

A deity-free working can be just as powerful as a planetary invocation.

A sigil-based ritual may be just as potent as a spirit-channeling session.

Hybrid workings—blending spirit contact, sigils, planetary forces, and raw energy—often generate the strongest results.

The only real limitation is hesitation.

Magicians who hesitate because they fear breaking from tradition or stepping outside established frameworks stunt their own power.

Magik bends to will.

It adapts to those who command it.

And those who learn to shape it without hesitation—become the system itself.

CHAPTER 4

The Role of Meditation in Magik

Meditation gets talked about like it's the ultimate solution to everything. If your magik isn't working, meditate. If your focus is off, meditate. If you struggle with visualization, meditate. While there's truth to this, not all meditation works for everyone. There's no universal method, and anyone claiming otherwise is just selling something. Meditation is a tool, and like any tool, its effectiveness depends on how well it fits the person using it.

Some people sit in a lotus position, close their eyes, and chant mantras. If that works for them, great. But for me, deep Theta meditation while lying down is what gets me into the right state. It slows everything down and shifts the mind into a space where magik flows effortlessly. For others, effective meditation might involve breathwork, walking meditations, or candle-gazing. The method itself isn't important—what matters is whether it gets results.

At its core, meditation is about training the mind to either focus with intensity on one thing or to enter a detached state where thoughts no longer disrupt the flow of energy. Magik requires focus. If your mind jumps from thought to thought, you're leaking energy before it even has a chance to build. That's where meditation comes in.

The Problem with Too Many Thoughts

I tend to let random thoughts creep in while I meditate. It doesn't matter how focused I am when I start—somewhere along the way, my brain decides it's time to analyze a conversation from three years ago, stress about whether I paid a bill, or suddenly remember the name of a song that was on the tip of my tongue last week. One of my guides likes to remind me that I have the attention span of a gnat, and honestly, they're not wrong.

This is where mindless meditation helps. Most people think meditation means clearing the mind completely, but that's not really the goal. The mind will always generate thoughts—that's its nature. The key isn't forcing silence but disconnecting from the thoughts themselves. Instead of actively trying to stop them, you let them pass without engaging.

Think of thoughts like a river. Most people try to stop the river from flowing, but that never works. Mindless meditation is about stepping back and watching the water move without getting pulled in. You don't chase thoughts; you don't follow them down rabbit holes—you just let them drift past.

This is easier said than done. The instinct is to react. A thought appears, and before you know it, you're inside it, reliving a memory, planning something, or overanalyzing. The trick is acknowledging the thought and letting it go before it pulls you in. This takes practice. You don't perfect it in a day, but the more you do it, the better you get at controlling where your attention goes and how long it stays there.

Mindless Meditation: How It Works

My other books, like Mind Magik, cover this, but it belongs here too. Mindless meditation isn't about emptying the mind—it's about detaching from thought completely. It's the difference between being caught inside the storm and standing back to watch the storm from a distance.

I do this best lying down, sinking into a deep Theta state, letting my awareness expand without attaching to anything. For me, this is far more effective than rigid meditation positions. My body relaxes, I let go completely, and the deeper the relaxation, the easier it is to slip into that space where thoughts lose their grip.

Thoughts still appear, but they don't stick. The mind becomes a passive observer rather than an active participant.

This is what makes it so effective for magik. If you can hold this level of detachment while working a ritual, the energy flows cleanly without mental interference—no second-guessing, no doubts, no scattered focus. Just pure intent.

Some people struggle with this because they feel like they should be actively doing something during meditation. That's the mistake. The whole point is to stop doing—to let the mind drift and allow awareness to expand without controlling it. This is where higher states of consciousness start opening up. It's where astral awareness begins. It's when the mind becomes a tool rather than a distraction.

Why Meditation Matters for Magik

Magik isn't about words, tools, or rituals. It's about directing energy with will. If your mind lacks discipline, your magik will be weak and scattered. Meditation isn't just about relaxation—it's mental training.

Without control over thought, rituals become unfocused, intent wavers, and energy gets lost. If you can't hold a single-pointed focus for more than a few seconds, how can you expect to channel the force of an invocation or direct a sigil's energy properly? Every aspect of magik depends on your ability to hold intention and direct power without interference. Meditation strengthens that ability.

It also teaches you how to enter altered states quickly. The deeper you go into meditation, the easier it becomes to shift consciousness on command. This is essential for everything from astral magik to trancework, invocation, and energy manipulation. If you can drop into an altered state in seconds, you don't need elaborate rituals to generate power. You become the ritual.

This is why so many systems emphasize meditation. But again, the method has to fit the magician. Forcing yourself into a meditation style that doesn't align with you will make it feel like a chore instead of a tool.

Choosing the Right Meditation for You

Some people prefer mantra meditation, repeating a word or phrase until the mind locks into rhythm. Others work best with breath-focused meditation, concentrating entirely on the inhale and exhale. Some prefer guided meditation, using visualization to direct the mind. None of these approaches are wrong, but they're not universal either.

For me, deep Theta meditation while lying down, in total stillness, works best. I let awareness expand without effort. But that might not work for you.

If you struggle to sit still without getting distracted, try a moving meditation—walking in a quiet place, focusing on each step, letting the body fall into rhythm. If you need an anchor for your focus, work with breath or steady background sounds. If you tend to fall asleep too easily, a more active method might be necessary.

The only right way to meditate is the way that trains your mind to enter a controlled, focused state effortlessly.

The First Step Toward Astral Magik

Everything in magik begins with the ability to shift consciousness at will. Meditation is the first step in that process. Before you can explore the astral, slip into altered states during ritual, or effectively invoke, evoke, or direct energy, you need to train your mind to quiet, detach, and focus.

Mindless meditation is the gateway to deeper work. It's how you step beyond the noise of thought and into direct experience. Once you can do this effortlessly, the doors to astral magik, spirit communication, and higher states of awareness open naturally.

Without mental control, astral work is unpredictable. With it, you can shift in and out of altered states at will, move between worlds without getting lost in distractions, and direct energy with precision. This is why meditation is the foundation of serious magik—not because it's a spiritual requirement, but because a disciplined mind is the most powerful tool a magician can have.

If you want to work higher-level magik, this is where you start. Not with rituals. Not with tools. But with the ability to enter the right state of mind instantly. When you can do that, everything else becomes easier.

Astral Travel: Unlocking the Gateway to Unlimited Power

The physical world is an anchor, but it is not a boundary. The real work of magik doesn't just happen in this reality—it happens between realities, in places most people never reach. The Astral Plane is where you test your power, expand your reach, and make contact with forces beyond what this world allows. Here, you can tap into hidden knowledge, build power structures, and move freely across unseen dimensions. Once you master this, nothing is out of reach.

A common mistake people make is assuming that the astral is just a dream space, a hallucination, or some kind of mental projection. It isn't. It's a real place—an actual plane of existence, separate from this one but deeply connected to it. The moment you step out of your body, you'll know this isn't just imagination. It's as real as the ground beneath your feet—maybe even more so.

Understanding the difference between the Astral Plane and the Mental Plane is crucial, as many people confuse the two. The Mental Plane is internal—it's the landscape of your own mind, filled with thoughts, projections, and subconscious structures. The Astral Plane is external—a space that exists beyond you, where entities, landscapes, and energy currents exist independently of your perception. The key is knowing when you're still navigating your own mental constructs and when you've actually stepped beyond yourself. That shift is what separates true astral travel from an overactive imagination.

How to Leave the Body at Will

Most people think astral travel is difficult. It isn't. The problem is that they try too hard. The more effort you put into forcing yourself out of your body, the more you reinforce the connection keeping you inside it. The trick is to relax completely while keeping your mind awake. The body falls away on its own. You don't have to push—you just have to let go.

The easiest way to do this is to bring yourself to the edge of sleep, that drifting state where you're not quite awake but not fully unconscious either. This is where the body naturally starts to disconnect. If you've ever woken up unable to move but fully aware, you've already reached the threshold. Sleep paralysis is the doorway to astral separation. Instead of fighting it, you learn to use it.

For me, the best way to separate is through deep Theta meditation while lying down. The body relaxes into near-sleep, but the mind stays sharp. You wait for that moment when your limbs feel numb, heavy, disconnected. That's when you shift. The key is to focus on a single point outside of yourself—not your body, not your breath, but something beyond. A floating sensation, a pull, an imagined movement. Your mind follows the motion, and before you realize it, you're already out.

HIGH MAGIK 303

The Anchor Method: Shifting in Under 5 Minutes

The biggest mistake people make when trying to leave their body is focusing too much on their body. The more you think about whether you're "out" yet, the more you reinforce the connection keeping you in. The Anchor Method solves this by shifting your awareness outside from the start.

Instead of trying to force separation, you anchor your awareness beyond your body. You pick a fixed point—a spot on the ceiling, a location across the room, or even just the sensation of movement upward. As your body begins to fade into relaxation, you shift all awareness to that point. You don't focus on leaving—you focus on already being there. The body lets go on its own.

This method works fast because it removes the struggle of "getting out." The more naturally you let the process unfold, the easier it becomes. You're not fighting to separate. You're following the same detachment process that occurs every time you sleep. The only difference is, this time, you remain aware.

Navigating the Astral Like a Pro

The first time you enter the Astral, it can feel disorienting. The rules of the physical world don't apply. There's no gravity, no linear sense of time. Space bends. If you think of a place, you're there. If you focus on a question, the answer manifests in some form. You'll see landscapes, structures, roads, tunnels—some feel solid and unchanging, while others shift and distort as you move through them.

Your own thoughts still have influence, especially in the first few minutes. This is where a lot of people get lost. They think of something, and it appears, leading them to assume the entire Astral Plane is just a projection of their mind. It isn't. The key is learning to distinguish between mental debris and actual astral structures. The more time you spend navigating the Astral, the clearer this becomes.

Not everything you encounter should be trusted. Some entities are just residual energy—thought-forms on autopilot, repeating old patterns. Others are conscious spirits, capable of communication and interaction. And some? Some should not be near you at all. If something feels off, leave immediately. The Astral isn't inherently dangerous, but it isn't entirely safe either. Your energy is your presence—if you feel strong, you are strong. If you feel weak, you are weak. Everything in the Astral reacts to your state of being.

The best way to navigate is with intention. If you drift aimlessly, you'll be pulled into whatever currents are nearby. But if you make a decision—set a location or goal—you'll find yourself there almost instantly. This is how you travel vast distances in seconds. Think it. Move. Arrive.

That's exactly what I do when I visit the Akashic Records, meet with a guide on their massive starship (no details here—it's private), or check out alien structures on the Moon or Mars.

Building Your Astral Temple

Most people treat the Astral like a place to visit. It's not. It's a place to build. (Okay, you can also meet up with people, test out the results of magik, the list is quite lengthy.)

An Astral Temple is a permanent structure you create in the Astral Plane, a place you can return to, shape, and use as a personal power center. Unlike the shifting landscapes of the general Astral, a Temple is your domain. Once it's built, it doesn't change unless you change it. It's a safe place, a base of operations, a sanctuary.

Why Building the Astral Temple Matters

Astral travel is more than just an escape from the physical. It's a gateway to power. The more you move between realities, the more control you have over both worlds. Information comes easier. Magik happens faster. You stop being bound by the limits of this plane. You start pulling power from beyond it.

Once you master this, everything changes. You no longer work magik in one world alone. You become a force moving through all of them.

Your Astral Temple

An Astral Temple isn't just a construct. It's a fixed point of power in a realm where most things shift and dissolve. The Astral itself is fluid. Landscapes change. Structures appear and vanish. Time moves strangely. Nothing is permanent unless you make it so. That's what separates a true Temple from everything else in the Astral—it isn't a place you find, it's a place you claim and build. When done right, it becomes unchangeable, untouchable, a personal fortress of knowledge, energy, and control. It doesn't erode like other parts of the Astral. It doesn't shift when you leave. It is yours, locked into place by will alone.

Finding the right location is the first step. Some places in the Astral feel dense, unstable, chaotic—always shifting, never still. Others feel like voids, empty and without form. Neither of these is ideal for a permanent structure. What you want is a space that feels solid, still, and undisturbed, a place where your energy won't be drowned out by residual forces. There are quiet places in the Astral, untouched spaces that seem to exist between everything else. When you come across one, you'll recognize it immediately. The energy will feel neutral, balanced, open for use. That's where you build.

Once you've found the right place, construction begins. Unlike the physical world, you don't stack bricks or carve stone. You form the structure directly from thought and will. The more detail you give it, the more solid it becomes. A vague idea of a room won't hold. A clearly defined chamber with walls, doors, symbols, and structure will. Every element should have a purpose. The foundation should be reinforced with your energy, anchored so deeply into the Astral that it cannot be moved or broken. Walls should be sealed against outside interference, doors locked to anything you don't personally allow inside. If you carve sigils into the design, make sure they serve a function—protection, energy amplification, stability. This is a permanent space. Every choice should be intentional.

Some spirits will offer to help construct it. Be careful with this. Some just want to attach themselves to a structure they didn't create, giving them easier access to your energy. If you build it yourself, it is fully yours. No outside interference.

An Astral Temple is more than just a refuge. It is a place of power, a gateway, a control center. The more time you spend inside it, the more it becomes an extension of you. Unlike most Astral locations, which exist independently, a properly built Temple is woven into your personal energy field. You don't just visit it—you carry it with you. Even when you aren't projecting, it remains anchored beyond time. This is what makes it indestructible. No external force can dissolve what has been fully integrated into your own structure.

Once built, your Temple can be used for more than just meditation or exploration. It becomes a library of hidden knowledge, a place where information is gathered, stored, and accessed at will. Knowledge flows differently in the Astral. Some of it exists as books, scrolls, or artifacts—tangible records that can be read and studied. Other knowledge exists as direct downloads—pure understanding absorbed in an instant. When you access something powerful, you need a place to keep it, a structure that holds and protects what you've uncovered. Without this, information can be lost. An Astral

Temple solves that problem. Everything you learn, everything you collect, can be placed here, stored beyond the limits of physical memory.

Energy storage is another key function. The Astral is full of raw power, currents of force that can be drawn in, shaped, and held. Most of it dissipates without form, lost the moment you leave. But inside a Temple, energy can be contained, refined, and used when needed. It can be infused into the walls, concentrated into objects, embedded into sigils. The Temple itself becomes a generator, a battery, a power source that strengthens over time. If you need to amplify a working, you don't have to pull from yourself. You draw from what's already been gathered. The more energy you store, the stronger the Temple becomes.

Some choose to keep spirits within their Temple. This is a careful decision. Not all spirits should be given access to a personal space of power. Some will offer assistance in exchange for being housed within the structure. Some will attach themselves without permission, drawn to the stability of a place that doesn't shift like the rest of the Astral. You must be deliberate in who or what is allowed inside. Any spirit housed within your Temple becomes a permanent fixture, and its presence will shape the energy of the space. If you allow something in, make sure it serves your will, not the other way around.

A well-constructed Astral Temple is a fortress, a sanctum, a library, and a power source all in one. It is a place that exists outside of time, always available, always under your control. It doesn't fade when you leave. It doesn't erode. It is a permanent extension of your will, existing beyond the limits of the physical world. If you ever needed proof that reality is something you can shape, your Temple is it. It is something that was never there before but now will always be.

Working a Ritual in the Astral

I work rituals in the Astral more often than I do in the physical. It's easier, faster, and in many ways, more potent. A physical ritual requires time, space, tools, and setup. An Astral ritual requires only the will to perform it. Once you understand how energy moves between planes, you realize there's no real difference between working a ritual in the physical world and working it in the Astral. The mechanics are the same. The focus, intention, and execution don't change. The only thing missing is the physical action—but that's never where the power came from, anyway.

Magik has always been about will and energy, not candles or incense. The purpose of the physical setup is to create an environment that aligns the mind and spirit with the working. When you step into the Astral, that environment is built instantly. There's no need to light a candle. The flame is already there the moment you decide it is. No need to carve a sigil into wax. The sigil is formed in energy the second you command it into existence. The Astral strips away the distraction of physical action and leaves you with pure intent, direct and unfiltered.

The first time you work a ritual in the Astral, it might feel strange. In the physical, there's a sense of weight, progression, tangible movement from step to step. In the Astral, everything happens at once. The circle is cast in an instant. The offering is presented the moment you think of it. The spirit is already present before the final words are spoken. There's no waiting. No delay. Reality moves at the speed of thought.

A ritual to Lilith is a good example. I've called on her in the Astral many times, and she always appears the same way—black leather jacket, bustier, a presence that fills the space immediately. There's no hesitation, no slow arrival. The moment I call her, she's there. That's another difference between the Astral and the physical. There's no need to build up energy, no gradual shift in atmosphere. In the Astral, the connection is instant.

The ritual itself is simple. I speak her name with intent, drawing her energy into the space. The setting shifts to match the working—a dark atmosphere, a presence like a storm on the horizon. I state my purpose clearly and directly. The power doesn't come from long invocations or complex wording. It comes from absolute clarity of intent. I see the result in my mind, feel it moving through the space, solidifying as something real. I present the offering—not physically, but through recognition. The actual offering comes later, in the physical, placed before her statue at the right time. The ritual closes with an acknowledgment of the exchange. In the physical, I might light a candle or burn a sigil. In the Astral, I seal the working with force of will, feeling the shift as the energy locks into place.

The moment it's done, it's done. There's no lingering doubt, no second-guessing. Astral rituals don't allow for hesitation. If the intent isn't strong, the energy doesn't move. If the call isn't real, the spirit doesn't come. Everything in the Astral is pure function—either it works, or it doesn't. If a ritual is weak, you know immediately. If it's powerful, the effects are felt instantly. That's why I prefer working rituals in the Astral. No delay. No unnecessary formality. Just direct contact, immediate results, and a level of magikal force that doesn't fade when you open your eyes.

Astral Weapons & Defense: Creating Tools for Protection in Non-Physical Realms

Magik doesn't stop at the physical. If we're operating in the Astral, working pathworkings, traveling realms, or engaging in high-level rituals, we need to take security just as seriously as we would in the material world. Protection isn't just about throwing up a shield and hoping for the best; it's about knowing how to defend, counter, and fortify ourselves in the unseen planes.

In the Astral, everything is thought-responsive, meaning whatever we create exists as long as we can maintain its structure. This is why astral weapons and defensive constructs are crucial tools. Unlike physical tools, these weapons are forged with focused intent, shaped by energy, and charged through visualization, repetition, and reinforcement.

Forging an Astral Weapon

Creating an astral weapon follows the same principle as forging a sigil or constructing a servitor—it's built from energy and purpose. The first step is deciding what kind of weapon you need. Do you need a sword to cut through bindings and negative attachments? A staff to direct energy and reinforce shields? A dagger for quick, precise work? A whip or chain to bind an entity? Whatever the choice, the key is clarity.

To craft your weapon:

- Enter an Alpha or Trance State: This allows your energy to stabilize, making it easier to pull from the surrounding astral material.
- Visualize the Energy Forming the Weapon: See it materializing in front of you. It should have weight, texture, and a distinct feel to it. The more details you can imagine, the more solid it becomes.
- Infuse it with Intent: This isn't just a visualization exercise; you are programming this weapon to serve a specific purpose. If you're creating a

sword, imagine it cutting through all illusions and energetic bindings. If it's a shield, see it deflecting all negative energy effortlessly.
- Charge it with Power: Call upon a deity, spirit, or planetary energy that resonates with protection. If working with a martial force like Mars, you can chant, "By the power of Mars, I forge this blade to defend and strike with precision." Let the energy flow into the weapon until it hums with power.
- Test the Weapon: Once created, practice using it in a controlled space. Swing it, thrust it, feel how it moves. In the Astral, the mind controls everything, so if the weapon feels sluggish or unresponsive, refine the process.
- Anchor It to Your Energy Field: This is what makes it last beyond a single use. Tether the weapon to your aura by visualizing it resting at your side when not in use. This allows you to summon it instantly when needed.

Once formed and charged, astral weapons remain a part of your spiritual arsenal. With continued use, they grow stronger and more responsive.

Astral Armor and Shielding

Weapons are one thing, but defensive measures are just as critical. You wouldn't go into a fight unarmored, so why would you explore the Astral without protection? The simplest defense is a shield, but a truly advanced practitioner takes it further by layering protection in multiple forms.

Basic shielding is done by visualizing a sphere of energy surrounding you, programmed to repel unwanted forces. But this is only the start. We can weave armor, reinforcing our energy bodies so we're not only defended but also resilient.

- The Mirror Shield: A reflective surface that sends any attack or unwanted energy back to its source. Ideal for dealing with malicious entities.
- The Elemental Shield: Using the elements to construct armor. Fire burns away negativity, Water absorbs and neutralizes, Earth grounds, and Air disperses.
- The Warding Sigil Armor: Inscribing sigils into an astral breastplate or cloak adds layers of programmed intent—wards that block specific entities or energy types.
- Light Weaving: Instead of heavy armor, weaving a flexible cloak of light allows for movement while still providing protection. This is good for those who want to remain undetected in certain astral spaces.

Like astral weapons, shielding and armor must be maintained. The more often you reinforce them, the stronger they become.

Charging Astral Objects and Bringing Their Power into the Physical World

Now, let's go deeper into charging astral constructs and making their power tangible in the material plane. This is the key to manifesting real-world results from the work we do in the Astral.

Astral objects—whether weapons, talismans, or constructs—exist as energy patterns in non-physical reality. Without proper anchoring, they fade over time. Charging these objects ensures they hold power and influence beyond the Astral. This absolutely works. I decided I wanted a new digital camera, so in the Astral, I picked out the camera, focused on how it felt in my hand, and made it fully real in the Astral. Then I charged it, as I outline below, and within a week, the camera was actually in my hands.

How to Charge an Astral Object

Charging an astral construct is similar to empowering a sigil or servitor. The goal is to imbue it with energy, reinforce its structure, and link it to a physical counterpart when needed.

Channeling Energy into the Object

Once an astral object is created, it needs a steady infusion of energy to stabilize. The easiest way is through focused intention and visualization, but adding external sources amplifies the process.

Methods include:
- Drawing power from celestial bodies (sunlight,

moonlight, planetary hours)
- Using breathwork (exhaling energy into the object)
- Chanting sacred words or deity names
- Invoking spirits to lend power to the object

<u>Linking It to the Physical World</u>

Astral constructs can be anchored to physical objects to maintain their influence. Therefore, certain tools—ritual daggers, charms, and sigils—hold more power when consistently used.

Choose a corresponding physical counterpart:
- An astral sword can be linked to an athame.
- A protective astral sigil can be bound to a pendant.
- A charged astral shield can be anchored to a piece of clothing or jewelry.

To merge the energies, hold the physical object while focusing on the astral counterpart. Will the energies to blend. You should feel a shift—heat, tingling, or heaviness—when the connection locks in.

<u>Charging Through Ritual and Offerings</u>

- Offerings of incense, fire, or blood (if appropriate) can be used to further charge and strengthen astral constructs.
- Speaking power words or mantras can lock in

- energy, ensuring longevity.
- Some spirits, particularly those governing magikal craftsmanship (like Hephaestus or Ptah), can be invoked to reinforce an astral weapon's permanence.

Activating and Recharging Over Time

Like physical tools, astral constructs lose power if neglected. Regular cleansing and recharging ensure they remain effective.

Placing them in ritual smoke, setting them in moonlight, or running specific visualizations re-energizes them.

If an astral construct begins to feel weaker, it likely needs an energy boost.

Bringing the Power into the Material World

Beyond linking astral tools to physical objects, the real key to making them effective in the waking world is through embodied action. This means aligning our physical choices with the energy we've programmed into the astral tool. If we create a weapon for protection, we need to carry ourselves with the confidence that we are shielded. If we forge an astral talisman for success, we must act in alignment with opportunities that manifest.

This is how we fully integrate the Astral with the material. Magik is not just about energy—it's about power put into motion.

David Thompson

With this understanding, astral weapons, defense, and charged objects become more than just theoretical tools. They become part of your real, functional magikal arsenal, fully connected to both the unseen and the material world.

CHAPTER 5

Time & Reality Manipulation

Time is not as rigid as people think. We grow up believing it flows in one direction—past to present to future, like a river with a fixed current. But the reality is far stranger. Time doesn't move in a straight line; it bends, it loops, it stretches, and it compresses. The ancients understood this. Magicians, mystics, and even some scientists today recognize that time is an elastic force, something that can be altered, manipulated, or even bypassed entirely.

This is why some moments stretch forever, while others slip by in an instant. Why time speeds up when we're caught in the thrill of life, and drags when we're waiting for something to happen. This is our first key to understanding time manipulation: perception. Time is subjective. It isn't just a measurement on a clock; it's something we experience. And because we experience it, we can change how it flows.

The Fluid Nature of Time

Time is a function of awareness. It is shaped by our focus, our emotions, and even the structure of reality itself. When we are deeply engaged, time condenses. This is why an hour spent in passion or deep conversation can feel like minutes, while a tedious task can stretch seconds into eternity. The more engaged our minds, the faster time seems to move. But the opposite is also true. When we focus intently on something, when we drop into deep presence, we can slow time.

This is something warriors and athletes instinctively understand. A fighter dodging a punch sees everything in slow motion. A runner in peak performance feels like they have all the time in the world to adjust their stride. This isn't an illusion. It's time dilation on a personal scale. When we fully engage, we expand the moment. It's not just in the mind—our nervous system, our entire consciousness, begins interacting with time differently.

In magik, this understanding is key. If we can shift our perception of time, we can change how it unfolds for us. We can stretch an opportunity, giving ourselves more time to act. We can compress long waits into the blink of an eye. More advanced techniques can even allow us to step outside the usual flow of time, seeing into futures and pasts that exist alongside the present.

How Time Can Be Altered

Altering time isn't about controlling the outside world directly. It's about shifting how we interact with the temporal field that surrounds us. There are three primary ways to manipulate time: **through intention, mental states, and energetic alignment.**

1: Intention

Intention is the foundation of all magik, and time manipulation is no different. Time moves where attention flows. If you hold the firm intention that time will stretch or contract, it does. This isn't wishful thinking—it's a focused act of will. The more skilled we become at controlling our awareness, the more we can exert influence over how time unfolds.

A simple example: when running late, instead of panicking, hold the intention that time will work in your favor. Many practitioners have experienced the odd phenomenon of arriving on time despite all odds, finding lights turn green, traffic opens, or people they were meeting were also delayed. This is an entry-level time shift—nudging reality so events align in your favor.

2: Mental States and Time Perception

The brain is a time machine. It filters and processes reality, determining how long or short any experience feels. Meditation and altered states of consciousness allow us to step outside of linear time. In deep trance, time ceases to exist in the way we normally experience it. This is why skilled practitioners can engage in astral journeys that feel like hours but take only minutes in the physical world.

One of the fastest ways to manipulate time is by shifting mental states. Entering a heightened state of awareness, such as flow or deep presence, allows us to slow things down. On the other hand, distracting the conscious mind can speed time up. This is why rituals, music, and rhythmic movements are used in magik—they alter our perception of time, and in doing so, they alter time itself.

3: Energetic Alignment and Time Warping

Every moment in time has a specific energy signature. By tapping into this, we can align ourselves with the flow of time that best serves us. Ancient magicians understood this through astrology—working magik at specific planetary hours to align their intent with the natural rhythms of time. But we don't need astrology to do this. We can sense time's currents and step into the right flow through practice.

If you've ever had a day where everything lines up perfectly—where you seem to be in sync with the universe, getting exactly what you need at exactly the right moment—you've touched this principle. The opposite is also true. When time works against us, when everything seems to slow and block us at every turn, we've fallen out of sync with time's natural flow. These are the moments when time manipulation is most needed—when we must step out of the chaotic currents and realign with a path of smooth unfolding.

The Practical Side of Time Magik

Once we understand that time can be influenced, we start to see its effects everywhere. We see how anticipation lengthens time, how fear and anxiety stretch moments into unbearable eternities, while joy and excitement make time vanish. We see how some people seem to move through life effortlessly, always in the right place at the right time, while others struggle as if constantly behind or out of sync.

By consciously working with time, we can begin shifting these patterns. We can compress time when waiting for something to manifest, making weeks feel like days. We can expand time to give ourselves more space for critical actions. And, with deeper work, we can begin stepping into non-linear time, where the past, present, and future are all accessible.

One of the first signs of successful time magik is synchronicity—the seemingly impossible alignment of events that work in your favor. This is time responding to intention. The more we work with time, the more we see that it isn't a rigid system—it's a living, breathing force, and it can be shaped.

This is only the beginning. True mastery over time involves deeper techniques—entering timeless states, jumping between probabilities, bending events so they occur exactly when they are most beneficial. But for now, understanding that time is fluid, and that we have the power to shape it, is enough. Time is not our master. It is a force we can wield.

The Magik of Probability

Probability is the undercurrent of reality. Every moment, every event, every outcome exists as a web of possibilities, some more likely than others. Magik isn't about defying probability outright—it's about tilting it. Shifting the weight of possibility so that what we desire becomes the most natural unfolding of reality. The smallest shift in probability can change everything. A missed opportunity becomes an open door. A stroke of luck appears where none should have been. Events realign, pulling you into a version of reality where things just seem to go your way.

Magicians have always understood this. The ancient world didn't see fate as fixed; it was something that could be influenced, shaped, bent. In our modern world, people unknowingly play with probability all the time. A gambler "gets hot" and wins streaks that defy logic. A person consistently finds themselves in the right place at the right time. Luck isn't random—it's probability bending, often unconsciously. Magik takes this a step further. Instead of waiting for chance to favor us, we work directly with the forces that shape probability, creating outcomes instead of hoping for them.

High Magik 303

Every possible outcome exists in the unseen realm before it becomes physical. This is why intent matters. Focused will, clear visualization, and emotional charge all act as forces that push one probability forward while suppressing others. Without magikal influence, events unfold in a default pattern based on existing conditions—past actions, environmental factors, and collective energy. When we apply magik, we override these defaults. We push reality toward a specific shape.

Probability shifts happen in subtle ways at first. A conversation opens a door that was previously closed. Someone who never noticed you before suddenly does. A financial opportunity appears where there was none. This is why synchronicity increases when working with magik. The more reality bends, the more we notice things lining up perfectly. It starts small—then cascades.

The key is understanding that probability isn't a single force but a field of interwoven factors. The past affects the present, and the present influences the future. When working with probability, we don't fight against the flow—we redirect it. If a situation is stacked against us, we don't force change through brute strength. We shift the conditions around it. A locked door doesn't need to be broken down if we can make someone open it from the other side.

This is why subtle magik often works better than overt force. A whisper to reality, a slight push in the right place, can collapse a series of probabilities into one inevitable outcome.

It's not about forcing something that was never meant to be—it's about making sure the path of least resistance leads exactly where we want to go. Reality already holds every possible outcome. We decide which one unfolds.

Jumping Timelines—How to Shift to a Better Version of Your Reality

This is a simplified breakdown of timeline shifting. I cover this in much greater depth in my Quantum Timeline class, where I go into the mechanics of alternate realities, shifting techniques, and the deeper processes behind how and why this works. But for now, let's focus on the essentials—how to recognize the version of reality you're in, how to shift into a better one, and how to ensure that shift holds.

Reality isn't a single, fixed path. Every moment, you exist within one of many possible versions of your life, each connected by an intricate network of probabilities. These timelines range from barely distinguishable variations—where a conversation plays out slightly differently—to radically different ones where your entire life takes another trajectory. Every decision you make shifts you, even slightly, onto a new path. Most people do this unconsciously, following default patterns. Magik gives us the tools to do it with intent.

Jumping timelines isn't about forcing a sudden, external shift where you wake up in an entirely different world. It's about stepping into the version of yourself that already exists within the reality you want. You shift your consciousness, align with the frequency of the new timeline, and as your mind and energy settle into that state, external reality follows.

Understanding How Timelines Work

Timelines are held in place by three main forces:

1. Your Identity – The version of yourself you believe yourself to be. If you see yourself as someone who struggles, you align with timelines where struggle is inevitable. If you step into the identity of someone who always finds a way, reality restructures itself around that belief.
2. Your Decisions – Every choice creates a split. Major decisions cause larger jumps, but even small actions shift the course of events. If you keep making the same choices, you stay on the same path. If you start disrupting patterns, new timelines open.
3. Your Emotional and Energetic State – Reality reflects the emotional frequency you hold. If you are deeply aligned with stress, doubt, or frustration, you are tuned to timelines where those conditions persist. If you shift your internal state—by training your focus, your emotions, and your beliefs—you shift to a version of reality where things play out differently.

How to Shift Timelines with Intent

To move to a better version of reality, you need to break the cycle of your current timeline and align with a new one. This requires two key elements: conscious choice and energetic immersion. Below are two exercises that accomplish this.

Exercise 1: Immersion Method – Becoming the Version of You That Already Exists

This method focuses on identity alignment—becoming the version of yourself that already exists in the timeline you want.

- Get Clear on the Timeline You Want.
- Close your eyes and strip away all distractions. Imagine a version of your life where everything is exactly how you want it to be.
- Focus on the you in that timeline. How do they think? How do they speak? How do they react to situations? How do they move through the world?

This version of you already exists. Your goal is to step into them.

Drop Into the New Identity

Still with your eyes closed, start shifting your posture, your breathing, and your mindset to match the version of you in the desired timeline.

If this version of you is confident, sit up straighter. If they feel financially abundant, feel that security settling into your body. If they have deep connections, feel the warmth of those relationships as if they already exist.

This isn't visualization—it's full immersion. You are no longer imagining; you are shifting.

Step Back Into Reality as the New You

Open your eyes, but do not mentally return to your old timeline. Carry the feeling, the posture, and the energy of the new you into your physical reality.

Every action from this moment forward should come from this version of yourself. If a decision needs to be made, ask yourself, what would the version of me in the new timeline do? and follow through.

The more you hold this shift, the more reality bends to match.

Exercise 2: Breaking the Old Timeline – Disrupting Patterns to Force a Shift

Timelines are held in place by routine. If you do the same things, react the same way, and think the same thoughts, you reinforce the same version of reality. To break into a better one, you need to disrupt your usual patterns.

Choose One Area of Your Life to Shift

Pick an area where you feel stuck—money, relationships, career, personal confidence.

Identify the patterns you repeat in this area. What choices do you make that keep reinforcing your current reality?

Disrupt the Pattern Immediately

Do something drastically different. Take a new route

home. Change the way you start your morning. Speak to someone you normally wouldn't.

The goal is to create a break in the pattern—something so different that it forces a realignment.

Even a small shift in action can create a ripple that leads to a new timeline.

Stack More Changes to Accelerate the Jump

Throughout the day, keep disrupting old patterns. If your usual habit is to hesitate, take bold action instead. If you normally doubt yourself, make a decision with complete certainty.

With each shift, the old timeline weakens, and the new one takes hold.

The key is repetition. The more you act in alignment with the new timeline, the faster the shift locks into place.

Holding the Shift So the New Timeline Becomes Permanent

Jumping to a new timeline is easy. Staying there is where most people fail. The moment you fall back into old patterns—old habits, old reactions, old self-doubt—you begin slipping back into the previous timeline. To hold the shift, you have to anchor it.

Reinforce the New Identity – Every morning, remind yourself of who you are now. Speak it, feel it, embody it.

Refuse to Engage With the Old Timeline – If an old challenge resurfaces, do not react as you would in the past.

Handle it as the version of you from the new timeline would.

Trust the Process – The moment you assume the shift didn't work, you collapse the new reality. Instead, assume that the shift is already in progress, and let the physical world catch up.

Why This Works

Timeline jumping is based on a mix of energy, psychology, and quantum principles. When you shift your identity and disrupt the old patterns, you force reality to realign. It has no choice but to match your internal state. This isn't just theory—it's something that can be tested.

Every shift starts small. A chance encounter. An unexpected opportunity. A decision that feels different than usual. Then the changes stack. A week from now, the energy has shifted. A month from now, the shift is undeniable. Reality moves because you moved first.

Timelines are not fixed. They are fluid, constantly shifting based on your focus, your actions, and your level of awareness. When you apply this consciously, you take control. You are no longer bound by fate or circumstance. You decide which version of reality you step into.

This is only the beginning. True mastery comes with practice, with layering techniques, with stacking probabilities so that every shift compounds. But even with these methods alone, you can break free from the limitations of your current timeline and step into something better. The version of reality you want already exists. Your job is to step into it and never look back.

Bending Time Ritual—Slowing Time Down or Speeding It Up

Time is fluid. It is not an external force moving at a fixed rate, but an experience shaped by perception, energy, and intent. You've already felt this—moments of deep focus where time stretched, or times of excitement when hours vanished in an instant. This ritual lets you control that experience, either slowing time when you need more of it or accelerating it when you want something to pass quickly.

This is a mental-only ritual. No tools, no external props. Just your mind, your will, and your ability to shift perception. Although, if you prefer, you can use a candle or incense. Totally up to you!

Step 1: Set the Intention

Decide whether you are slowing time down or speeding it up. Be precise. You're not manipulating all of time—just your personal experience of it within a set moment.

- To slow time: Use this when you need more time for a task, to extend a pleasurable experience, or to make a single moment feel longer.
- To speed time up: Use this when waiting for something, pushing through a dull moment, or wanting to accelerate an event's arrival.

- State the intent clearly in your mind:
- "I stretch this moment, expanding time so that every second feels fuller."
- "I contract this moment, speeding up time so this experience passes swiftly."

The command should be firm. No hesitation. Your mind dictates how time unfolds for you.

Step 2: Enter the Field of Time Perception

Close your eyes. Take three deep breaths. Let your awareness shift away from the outside world and into the sensation of time itself.

Feel the weight of time around you. Is it heavy and slow? Light and fleeting?

Imagine time not as a clock but as a substance—like a river, an ocean, or threads woven around you.

Hold the feeling that time is something you can touch, mold, and command.

This step is important. The more tangible time feels, the easier it is to manipulate.

Step 3: Alter the Flow of Time

Now, reshape the experience.

Slowing Time (Expanding the Moment)
- Imagine the space around you widening. The room expands. The air becomes heavier, denser. Everything slows.

- Picture a thick golden light stretching across your vision, elongating everything it touches.
- Breathe deeply and count slowly in your mind. Feel the gap between seconds expand. Time responds to your pace.
- Lock it in by thinking: "Time is vast. I move through it with ease. Each moment stretches to hold all I need."
- You'll feel an internal shift—everything slows, awareness deepens, time stretches.

Speeding Time (Contracting the Moment)

- Imagine the space around you collapsing inward. The room shrinks. The air becomes lighter. Everything compresses.
- Picture time as a fast-moving current, flowing around you at double speed.
- Breathe quickly but steadily. In your mind, shorten the gaps between seconds, making them flicker past faster.
- Lock it in by thinking: "Time is swift. I move through it effortlessly. This moment contracts and passes in a blink."
- You'll notice a mental shift—awareness lightens, and time begins to slip by faster.

Step 4: Hold the Shift

For the next few minutes, stay in the altered perception. Do not check a clock. Time bends according to experience, and checking external time can snap you back into its default state. Instead, stay fully engaged in the moment and let the shift hold naturally.

If you slowed time, you'll feel everything deepen, as if moving through honey.

If you sped time up, you'll feel like events are skipping ahead, moving effortlessly.

Once you feel the shift is stable, release the focus and return to normal awareness. The effect will continue to hold as long as you do not question it.

This works because time is subjective. The brain processes time based on perception, and by shifting focus, we override its default settings. With practice, this becomes second nature. You can slow time during intense moments, stretch the minutes of a ritual, or speed through waiting periods effortlessly.

Time bends when you decide it does.

Programming Reality Through Symbolism

Reality is built on symbols. Every culture, every language, every belief system is a network of symbols that encode meaning into the world. These symbols don't just represent ideas; they influence the way we think, the way we act, and the way reality unfolds around us. The subconscious processes symbols as commands. The right symbols, repeated in the right way, act as programming codes, shaping reality beneath conscious awareness.

Magicians, mystics, and even corporations understand this. Religious icons, ancient sigils, corporate logos—each one carries an energy, a meaning that imprints itself onto the mind and the external world. Numbers work the same way. Repeated sequences of numbers appear in moments of synchronicity, signaling a shift in probability, an alignment with a particular current of reality. These are not random. They are patterns, markers of where consciousness is directed, indicators of the timeline you are on.

When a specific number, symbol, or sign begins appearing repeatedly in your life, it is either an external confirmation of an existing shift or an invitation to reinforce one. A repeating number sequence—on a clock, a receipt, a street sign—is not just a coincidence. It is a moment where reality highlights itself, offering you a glimpse at the undercurrent shaping your path. If you respond to these symbols with intent, they become amplifiers, strengthening the probability of the desired outcome.

This is why certain symbols hold power across cultures. The ouroboros, the infinity loop, the cross, the pentagram—each has been embedded with meaning for centuries. Whether seen in a dream, carved into stone, or casually appearing on a billboard, their presence influences perception and shifts the mind toward specific patterns of thought. Those thoughts, when reinforced, shape reality.

Numbers function the same way. In magik, numbers are codes, each carrying a frequency that can be harnessed to adjust outcomes. The number three amplifies creation, movement, and expansion. Four stabilizes, grounds, and locks energy into place. Seven holds an esoteric current, connected to cycles, completion, and the deeper aspects of reality. When these numbers begin appearing consistently, they indicate a pattern forming beneath the surface. A person seeing repeated sevens is aligning with deeper knowledge, whether they are aware of it or not. Repeated ones indicate a reset, the opening of new pathways, an invitation to choose a direction.

Most people ignore these moments, writing them off as meaningless. But magicians recognize them as opportunities. When a symbol or number pattern appears, engaging with it reinforces the shift. A repeated number can be acknowledged as a confirmation and mentally locked in: Yes, this is the correct path, let it strengthen. A symbol that appears frequently can be integrated into a personal sigil, carrying its energy into future workings.

The mind thrives on repetition. What is repeated embeds itself into reality. This is why advertising works, why mantras hold power, why prayers are said in rhythmic patterns. It is also why certain numbers and symbols appear right before a significant change. They are not just reflecting the shift; they are pushing it forward. When you notice them, they are already affecting you. Choosing to work with them rather than ignore them amplifies the effect, turning a passive signal into an active force shaping your reality.

The key is to program reality before it programs you. Instead of waiting for signs, use them deliberately. Choose numbers that align with your goals and repeat them. Write symbols into existence through sigils, markings, or mental visualization. Engage with repeating patterns as if they are already shaping the outcome, because they are. Reality follows what is reinforced. The more you encode a message into it, the more it manifests.

The Observer Effect

Reality shifts under observation. This isn't just mystical theory—it's a fact backed by quantum physics. The Observer Effect, one of the strangest and most well-documented phenomena in quantum mechanics, shows that the mere act of observing changes the outcome of an event. In the famous double-slit experiment, electrons behave as both waves and particles, existing in a state of probability until measured. The moment they are observed, they collapse into a single outcome. This means reality does not fully form until it is witnessed. Conscious attention locks potential into matter, selecting one possibility from an infinite field.

Modern physics brushes against what magicians and mystics have always understood. Consciousness directs reality. What you observe, what you focus on, dictates what solidifies. Quantum mechanics describes it in terms of probability waves collapsing into a single measurable event, but on a practical level, this is how all of reality works. The more attention something receives, the more defined it becomes. The unseen remains fluid, existing in potential, while the observed becomes real.

Zen philosophy carries this understanding even further. In Zen, focus and attention determine energy flow. Where awareness rests, energy moves, and where energy moves, reality shifts. This is why meditation, concentration, and deliberate focus are considered pathways to enlightenment. By mastering attention, one masters reality. When the mind fixates on fear, the energy reinforces that experience. When it lingers in a state of stillness, reality settles into clarity. When it focuses on a goal with unwavering certainty, conditions begin arranging themselves to make that goal inevitable.

Magik functions within this same principle. Rituals are not just about words or symbols—they are tools for directing attention with precision. Spells work not because of the ingredients used, but because they act as anchors for focus, strengthening intent and keeping awareness fixed on the desired outcome. This is also why scattered or unfocused desires rarely manifest. If attention drifts, if doubt fractures the clarity of an intention, the probability of success collapses. A divided mind creates weak reality shifts. A focused one bends probability in its favor.

This also explains why observation alone can change an outcome. When you fixate on something—whether a goal, an event, or a person—the energy of your observation exerts a subtle influence. The more intensely you focus, the stronger the effect. This is why people who expect failure often encounter it. Their attention continuously reinforces that possibility until reality reflects it back. Conversely, those who expect success and refuse to acknowledge any other outcome seem to experience an effortless unfolding of events. They are not just lucky. They are aligning reality through the force of unwavering observation.

This effect is everywhere. It explains why luck follows those who assume things will work out. Why negativity compounds in people who constantly expect the worst. Why the moment you start looking for something, you begin seeing it everywhere. The mind acts as a filter, selecting which parts of reality become tangible and which remain in the background. This is the essence of conscious manifestation. When you deliberately control what you observe, what you focus on, you shape what becomes real.

The simplest application of this is refining awareness. Train yourself to observe what you want to grow rather than what you fear. Fix your attention on desired outcomes instead of unwanted possibilities. The more something is seen, the more it exists. The more it exists, the stronger its presence in reality. By controlling observation, you control manifestation. The universe is not solid. It is fluid, responding to the eyes that witness it. The moment you understand this, you stop reacting to reality and start shaping it.

CHAPTER 6

Developing Pathworking

Pathworking is an essential skill in high magik, allowing practitioners to establish direct, structured contact with spirits for the purpose of guidance, wisdom, and empowerment. Unlike simple meditative journeys or visualization exercises, pathworking requires an active engagement with a spirit to uncover insights beyond one's personal knowledge. This practice has been utilized for centuries by mystics, magicians, and spiritual seekers to access higher realms, unlock hidden knowledge, and develop their personal power.

In this chapter, I'll cover the fundamentals of pathworking: how to contact a spirit, channel the pathworking experience, and interpret the received messages. The focus will be on providing only the necessary tools and instructions while avoiding unnecessary complexity. While advanced practitioners may engage in intricate, multi-layered pathworkings, this chapter will serve as a streamlined guide for those beginning their journey into spirit-led exploration.

Before proceeding, it is important to emphasize that pathworking is not a casual endeavor. Unlike standard meditation, which is primarily an internal experience, pathworking involves engaging with external entities. This requires a certain level of telepathic reception and discernment. If your telepathic abilities are underdeveloped, you may find the process frustrating or ineffective. Spirits communicate in a variety of ways—through images, impressions, emotions, or even direct words. Recognizing these subtle forms of communication is crucial to successfully receiving and interpreting messages.

Approaching pathworking with the right mindset is also essential. This is not just an exploration of the subconscious mind, but a bridge between the practitioner and the spiritual realms. For this reason, it is imperative to enter into pathworking with respect, patience, and an open yet discerning mind. Rushing the process or forcing outcomes can lead to misleading experiences. With consistent practice, pathworking will become a valuable tool in your magikal arsenal.

Choosing a Spirit for Pathworking

Selecting the right spirit for your pathworking is one of the most crucial steps in the process. Spirits vary in nature, personality, and intent, making it essential to work with one that aligns with your needs and experience level. The spirit you choose will shape the nature of the pathworking, influencing the knowledge and insights you gain. Some spirits are highly communicative and willing to teach, while others are more elusive or require specific conditions to engage with them effectively.

Considerations for Choosing a Spirit

- Intended Purpose – Are you seeking guidance on a specific problem? Do you need clarity regarding a life decision? Different spirits specialize in different areas, such as wisdom, protection, love, or manifestation.
- Energetic Compatibility – Some spirits resonate naturally with certain individuals. If a particular spirit keeps appearing in your thoughts, dreams, or divination readings, this could be an indication that they are open to working with you.
- Your Level of Experience – Beginners should start with spirits known for their benevolence and willingness to guide, such as deities associated with knowledge and wisdom. Avoid spirits with volatile or trickster-like qualities unless you have advanced discernment skills.
- Previous Connections – If you have previously felt drawn to a particular deity, angel, or ancient being, consider deepening that relationship through pathworking. Familiarity often leads to clearer communication.

If you do not already have a spirit in mind, meditation or divination techniques, such as tarot or the pendulum, can help clarify which being is most suited for your pathworking. Keep in mind that spirits sometimes choose the practitioner rather than the other way around. If you begin seeing symbols, names, or signs related to a particular entity in your daily life, it may be a sign that they are reaching out to you.

The Role of Telepathy in Pathworking

Unlike the passive experience of a typical guided meditation, pathworking is a vibrant, interactive process; it's a dynamic exchange where you actively engage in a conversation with the spirit you have selected. In contrast to passive visualization, which is solely based on self-generation, pathworking involves an interactive process in which there is a mutual exchange of impressions, messages, and guidance between the practitioner and the spirit. One must recognize that passively imagining a scene or a deity is inadequate; a more active and involved approach is necessary for true understanding.

Developing the Sensitivity to Recognize Spirit Communication

Spirits communicate in many ways, often subtly at first. Their messages may come through fleeting thoughts, sudden emotions, or images that appear in your mind's eye. Understanding how these messages manifest is crucial to effectively engaging in pathworking.

- Clairvoyant Messages – Some practitioners experience vivid images in their mind's eye, ranging from symbols to fully developed scenes. These are often delivered as flashes or slow-building visions.
- Clairaudient Messages – Others may hear words, phrases, or sounds internally. These can be indistinguishable from one's own thoughts, requiring discernment to separate external communication from self-generated ideas.
- Clairsentience (Feeling the Spirit's Presence) – Many magicians describe a sudden change in energy, a tingling sensation, or a shift in the atmosphere when a spirit is near.
- Emotional Downloads – Some spirits transmit information as strong feelings or sudden realizations rather than direct words or images.
- Sudden Insights – At times, knowledge seems to "drop" into your awareness as a complete understanding, bypassing logical thought processes altogether.

Training Telepathic Reception for Pathworking

Pathworking success depends on the practitioner's ability to receive and translate spirit communication. Developing telepathic sensitivity is essential to distinguishing between genuine spirit messages and mental noise.

1. Mental Quieting Techniques – Before attempting pathworking, practice clearing the mind of unnecessary thoughts. Meditation techniques such as mindfulness and breathwork can help achieve the necessary mental stillness.
2. Focused Listening – Spend time daily focusing on subtle mental shifts. Notice how thoughts appear and identify which ones feel external versus those generated by your own mind.
3. Symbol Recognition – Spirits often use symbolic language. Keep a personal lexicon of images, colors, and sensations that repeatedly appear in your workings.
4. Dialoguing with the Spirit – During early interactions, ask simple yes/no questions and note how responses manifest. Do you hear an internal voice, feel a shift in energy, or see a symbolic response?
5. Validating Received Messages – Cross-check information gained during pathworking with external divination tools such as tarot or the pendulum. Consistency in received messages indicates genuine communication.

As your telepathic skills improve, you will become more adept at distinguishing the nuances of spirit communication. Over time, spirits will recognize your ability and respond in clearer, more direct ways, enhancing the depth and accuracy of your pathworkings.

High Magik 303

I'm a natural medium, and I have trained myself extensively over the course of my life, so I can experience all the possible ways a spirit will communicate. But that me, I don't expect everyone to be able to do this. Just keep at it.

Do's and Don'ts of Pathworking

Do's:
- Approach with genuine intent and respect.
- Keep a detailed record of experiences.
- Verify messages through additional means.
- Maintain a distraction-free environment.
- Work with spirits you feel comfortable with.

Don'ts:
- Avoid rushing the process.
- Do not assume all messages are literal—symbolism plays a key role.
- Refrain from forcing communication; let the spirit engage at its own pace.
- Never assume all spirits are benevolent—always practice discernment.

Pathworking Ritual Exercise

<u>Items Needed:</u>
- White candles (4 for each cardinal direction, plus 1 for the spirit)
- Frankincense incense
- An offering (wine, honey, or another appropriate

item)
- A fireproof bowl
- A written petition

Ritual Steps:
- Prepare the Space: Arrange candles and light the incense to cleanse the area.
- Light candles, then turn off the room lights.
- Cast the Circle: Use your preferred circle casting technique, visualizing a barrier forming.
- Invoke the Spirit: Use a researched invocation.
- State Your Petition: Clearly express your intent.
- Enter the Pathworking: Meditate and let the spirit guide you.
- Receive the Messages: Pay close attention to details.
- Offer Gratitude: Place the offering near the central candle.
- Close the Ritual: Extinguish candles in reverse order, release energy, and properly dispose of offerings.

I've practiced pathworking for years. It's my preferred method of working a fast, informal ritual when I have little time for a formal ceremony, particularly when dealing with spirits I know well. Over time, I have learned to refine my approach, recognizing the subtle shifts in energy that signal a spirit's presence and engagement. Pathworking has allowed me to maintain strong, ongoing connections with these entities, making it an invaluable tool in my magikal practice. Through this method, I can seek guidance, receive insights, and experience powerful transformations without the need for extensive preparation.

Pathworking is a profound technique that, when practiced correctly, can lead to deep spiritual insights and transformative experiences. It serves as a bridge between the mundane and the mystical, granting access to higher wisdom and unseen forces. The key to mastering this skill lies in patience, consistency, and a willingness to trust both yourself and the spirit you are working with. Over time, you will find that the more you engage in pathworking, the more natural and effortless the process becomes. Eventually, it will integrate seamlessly into your magikal workings, allowing you to call upon the wisdom of the spirits as easily as you would consult an old friend. Through this practice, you will develop a heightened sense of spiritual awareness, an enriched connection to the divine, and a powerful tool for shaping your path in magik and beyond.

CHAPTER 7

A Personal Grimoire

Sometimes referred to as a "Book of Shadows," the concept of keeping a written record of magikal work goes back centuries, to a time when magik was truly occult—meaning hidden. Practitioners carefully guarded their knowledge, keeping it from prying eyes, only sharing with trusted allies, initiates, or clients. But secrecy wasn't just about tradition. It was a survival tactic in a world where magik was often persecuted. Today, for the most part, we no longer have to conceal our practice from religious authorities, but the importance of a magikal journal remains. It's the single most effective way to track progress, refine techniques, and establish personal correspondences with spirits, energies, and the very fabric of reality itself.

A living grimoire is more than just a collection of rituals and spells. It is a working document of a magician's journey, a record of successes, failures, and unexpected insights. It bridges the gap between personal experience and universal magikal principles, evolving as the practitioner deepens their understanding. Unlike historical grimoires—rigid texts often copied word for word through generations—this book is alive, responding to your path and refining itself through your work.

I keep two separate journals: one for my personal workings, and another for notes that eventually make their way into books like this one. Over the years, I've amassed a collection ranging from cheap spiral-bound notebooks to high-quality Leuchtturm1917 hardcover journals. I prefer the dot-grid format, which offers structure without restricting freeform notes or sketches. While the medium is personal preference, the key is consistency. A living grimoire grows with you, revealing patterns in your practice that might otherwise be overlooked.

The Science Behind Recording Magik

Recording rituals isn't just about documentation; it's a key part of shaping reality. Modern neuroscience tells us that writing things down reinforces neural pathways, embedding knowledge deeper into the subconscious. Quantum physics adds another layer to this: observation affects reality. The famous double-slit experiment demonstrates that the act of measuring particles changes their behavior. In magik, this principle translates to focus—where attention goes, energy flows. By writing down our magikal work, we are not only tracking progress but reinforcing our intent in a tangible way. It's a form of magikal observation, anchoring energy into the material world.

The Zen masters understood this principle long before quantum mechanics provided a scientific framework. They teach that the mind directs energy, and where focus is placed, reality shifts. The same applies to magik: our will, channeled through deliberate attention, affects the subtle fabric of reality. A living grimoire is not just a journal—it's a tool for refining focus, directing energy, and strengthening the will.

How to Structure Your Grimoire

There's no universal template, but certain elements make a grimoire more effective:

Record Every Ritual – Whether successful or not, every working should be documented. Note the spirits summoned, the specific intent, and any deviations from the original plan. Small details can later reveal why some rituals work and others falter.

Track Astrological and Environmental Factors – Even if you don't consciously time rituals with celestial alignments, noting the moon phase, planetary hour, or any unusual environmental factors (storms, power outages, personal mood shifts) can provide valuable insights.

Include Channeled Messages – Spirits communicate in ways that often seem cryptic at first. Writing down every detail of a vision, message, or sudden realization ensures that nothing is lost. Over time, themes emerge that deepen understanding.

Refine and Adapt Rituals – Magik isn't static. The same ritual performed five years apart may require adaptation based on your evolved understanding. Recording these refinements prevents stagnation and allows continuous improvement.

Personal Symbols and Sigils – Developing your own symbols rather than relying solely on traditional ones strengthens your personal connection to the work. Include sketches, automatic writing, and spontaneous sigils that emerge during deep meditative states.

Dreams, Omens, and Synchronicities – Often, messages from the subconscious or spirits appear outside ritual space. Keeping track of dreams, repeating symbols in daily life, and seemingly random insights will often tie back into your work in unexpected ways.

The Power of Writing Magik Into Reality

Magik is not just performed; it is built, tested, and refined over time. A grimoire allows you to see where patterns emerge, which spirits respond best to your calls, and which methods yield the strongest results. More than that, it becomes a testament to your journey. Each word written carries the weight of intent, forming a deeper connection between thought and manifestation.

By keeping a living grimoire, we solidify our place within the great web of reality. We record not just our personal progress but contribute to the evolving legacy of magikal practice. Whether handwritten in a simple notebook or digitized for reference, the key is commitment.

Magik is about directing energy, and a grimoire ensures that energy flows with clarity, precision, and purpose.

A grimoire isn't just a book filled with rituals and spells; it's a living, breathing magikal entity. Unlike a standard journal or reference manual, a grimoire carries the weight of your intent, the energy of every working, and the imprint of the spirits and forces you interact with. Every word written, every sigil drawn, every page turned shapes its power. Over time, it transforms from a collection of notes into a nexus of energy, a companion in your magikal journey that actively responds to your work.

The moment ink meets paper, the grimoire starts to accumulate power. Thoughts become symbols, symbols become patterns, and patterns weave together to create a reality all their own. Writing in it isn't just recording—it's an act of manifestation. The very act of documenting rituals, insights, and experiences binds them more tightly into your subconscious, reinforcing your magikal growth. This is why grimoires are treated with reverence. They are not static books; they are evolving constructs that deepen and refine your magikal abilities with every entry.

High Magik 303

The energy a grimoire holds comes from more than just your writings. Every interaction, whether through ritual use, meditation, or simple reflection, builds an ongoing dialogue between you and the forces you work with. A well-used grimoire carries an imprint of your past workings, creating a resonance that makes future rituals more potent. Spirits recognize it. Patterns emerge in its pages that might not have been obvious at the time of writing but later reveal connections you hadn't consciously seen. This is the nature of a magikal entity—it grows beyond its initial form, becoming something greater than the sum of its parts.

Over time, a grimoire begins to take on an almost autonomous presence. It will guide you as much as you guide it. There will be times when flipping through its pages will reveal exactly what you need to see, a synchronicity that speaks to its growing awareness of your path. Some magicians even report their grimoires behaving in peculiar ways—certain pages refusing to stay open, ink that darkens over time, an inexplicable sense of warmth or energy emanating from it. Whether this is simply the weight of intent or something more, the fact remains that a grimoire, when properly nurtured, takes on a life of its own.

This is why creating a grimoire is never just an intellectual exercise. It requires commitment, energy, and a willingness to allow it to evolve alongside you. It cannot be treated like an ordinary book, neatly organized and finalized. It must remain fluid, adaptable, ready to shift as your understanding deepens.

The moment a grimoire becomes rigid and lifeless, it stops being an active participant in your work and becomes nothing more than a historical record. That is the difference between keeping notes and maintaining a living grimoire.

A true grimoire bridges the gap between knowledge and practice, between idea and execution. It reflects not just what you know but what you are becoming. When crafted with awareness, it becomes a focal point for energy, a vessel for your intent, and a means of refining your connection to the unseen. It is an artifact of your own making, one that contains the pulse of your journey, ready to serve as a conduit for deeper power every time you turn the page.

This is why a grimoire is more than a simple record—it is an extension of the magician themselves. Every time you open it, you engage with its evolving energy, reinforcing the connection between your will and the forces you work with. The act of writing, sketching sigils, recording insights, and reflecting on past workings weaves it into your personal current of power. It is not merely an object; it is a living extension of your magikal self, shaping and being shaped in return.

A grimoire also acts as an anchor for intention. Each time you open it, you reinforce the link between thought and manifestation. This is why it's crucial to treat it with the same respect you would give to a sacred tool. Many magicians find that their grimoires develop an energy of their own, even influencing their practice by revealing forgotten wisdom or urging new directions. When properly used, a grimoire does not merely document—it transforms, amplifies, and refines the very workings it records.

The interplay between a magician and their grimoire is deeply personal. Some practitioners bless their books, charging them under specific planetary influences or binding them with protective sigils. Others allow their books to evolve naturally, absorbing the energy of their surroundings. There is no single right way—only what resonates with you. What matters is that the grimoire remains an active force in your magikal path, not a passive collection of words.

A grimoire is never truly finished. Even when a book is filled, the knowledge within continues to influence new workings, new books, and new expansions of power. Each volume becomes part of an ongoing dialogue between the magician and the currents of the unseen world. When properly nurtured, a grimoire stands as both a record of past experience and a guide toward future mastery.

Living Grimoire

A living grimoire must be more than a passive repository of knowledge. It should be designed to evolve, adapting to your path, absorbing the energy of your workings, and strengthening the connection between your intent and the forces you channel. The process of creation matters as much as the content itself. The materials, the ink, the binding—all of it plays a role in ensuring that the grimoire becomes an extension of your will, a personal artifact infused with power that grows alongside you.

To fully bind a grimoire to your energy, the process should begin before the first word is written. A blank book holds potential, but it is unfocused, neutral. Charging it, dedicating it, and linking it to your personal current ensures that it becomes more than paper and ink. One of the oldest and most potent ways to accomplish this is through blood. Blood is the essence of life, a physical manifestation of one's connection to the material and spiritual realms. A single drop, pressed into the cover, mixed into the ink, or traced into a sigil within its pages, can form an unbreakable link between you and the book. It marks it as yours, attunes it to your essence, and ensures that no one else can wield its full power.

Sigils further enhance this binding process. A grimoire should contain more than just instructions; it should hold coded power. Crafting a sigil that represents your magikal self—whether derived from your name, intent, or personal symbols—creates a unique seal that sets the tone for everything the book will contain. This sigil, when placed on the first page, the inside cover, or the book's spine, acts as a guardian and amplifier of the work within. Charging it with breath, intent, or even fire solidifies the connection between the grimoire and its creator.

Ink, too, carries significance. Traditional magicians often made their own, blending plant extracts, ashes, or even bodily fluids to create inks with specific energetic properties. Today, while modern inks work well, there is power in taking the extra step to charge them. This can be done through consecration, infusing the ink with intent before writing, or even mixing in trace elements of materials aligned with your workings. An ink laced with a single drop of your blood, or steeped in herbs sacred to your practice, ensures that every word carries not just meaning but energy.

A personalized grimoire evolves because it is never static. As your path unfolds, so too should the book. Some pages will become more potent over time, some entries will need revision as deeper truths are uncovered. Ritual pages, sigil sections, and recorded communications with spirits gain layers of resonance through repeated use. The more a grimoire is handled, read, and written in, the stronger its connection becomes. This is why it is crucial to let it grow, allowing new insights to reshape old entries and fresh energy to integrate into its pages. A living grimoire should never be viewed as a completed work; it is always in motion, shifting in tandem with its creator's unfolding path.

CHAPTER 8

Magikal Experimentation & Psychic Development

So, guess what happens when one practices magik for a while. I mean, aside from getting good at the magik part.

If you guessed "Become psychic?" then you're off to a good start.

First, let's take a look at how to experiment and test magik, like a scientist. I take this pretty far, myself, as I will wear a white lab coat while testing rituals. You don't need to do that.

Magikal experimentation is an essential part of becoming a skilled practitioner. It's not enough to just perform a ritual and hope for the best—you need to treat your magik like a scientist, testing it, refining it, and tracking results with

High Magik 303

precision. Without that level of discipline, you're just throwing energy into the void and hoping something sticks. The difference between a dabbler and a true magician lies in their ability to measure what works, adjust what doesn't, and push their limits based on real, tangible results.

To test your magik effectively, you need a system for tracking outcomes. A grimoire or magikal journal is crucial. Every time you perform a ritual, you should be recording the date, time, moon phase, planetary hour (if applicable), and what you did, down to the smallest details. The more information you have, the easier it is to spot patterns later. If your spells for financial gain always seem to work better during a waxing moon on a Thursday, that's something you can use to your advantage. If a ritual performed at midnight gives stronger results than one done at noon, you need to take note. Precision is what transforms guesswork into knowledge.

One mistake people make is assuming magik is instant or unpredictable. It's neither. A ritual sets energy into motion, but the manifestation process follows rules. Sometimes the effects are quick, other times they build over days or weeks. This is why tracking is so important. If a spell for attraction starts showing results in 10 days consistently, that's an observable trend. If a protection ritual weakens after a month, you now know how long its effects last. Without writing it down, you won't remember—memory is unreliable when dealing with subtle energy shifts. The key is to be as detailed as possible. Did you feel an energy shift after the ritual? Did anything unusual happen in dreams or daily life? Even minor synchronicities can be signals that something is in motion.

Testing also means refining techniques. Rocket engineers know this. They purposely test to failure. Failure tells them MORE than a success. A spell that only half-works isn't a failure—it's data. If a money ritual brings in unexpected side jobs instead of direct cash, that tells you something about how your energy is aligning with your intent. You can adjust by being more specific in your petition or tweaking your offerings. The scientific method applies to magik just as it does to any other field of study. You form a hypothesis (if I do X, then Y will happen), you test it (perform the ritual), you collect data (track the results), and you refine based on observations. If a technique fails outright, that's also valuable information—it means something in your execution, timing, or intent needs to be adjusted.

Another part of treating your magik like a science is eliminating variables when testing a new technique. If you change too many things at once, you won't know what actually caused the result. If you're testing a ritual for better communication, don't also change your social habits at the same time—that muddies the results. Keep the ritual consistent and then analyze what happens. If the results aren't what you expected, tweak only one element at a time—maybe change the incense, adjust the wording of your petition, or shift the timing. This way, you isolate what's actually making the difference.

Precision doesn't mean rigidity, though. Some of the best breakthroughs come when you experiment outside your usual methods. If you always use a certain summoning method but decide to try automatic writing instead, you might discover an entirely new way of working with a spirit. But the point is to test it properly, with structure and notes, so that if it works, you can replicate it.

Finally, the most important part of tracking magik is being brutally honest with yourself. Wishful thinking won't make a failed ritual successful. If something doesn't work, don't rationalize it—dig into why. Did you lack focus? Was your energy scattered? Were there external forces interfering? If you approach magik with the mindset of a scientist, every failure is just another step toward mastery. The more you track, test, and refine, the stronger your magik becomes.

Telepathy and spirit communication are skills that develop with practice. They aren't supernatural gifts handed down at birth, but abilities anyone can refine. The key is learning to recognize and separate external transmissions from your own internal dialogue. Most people assume telepathy means hearing words in your head like a conversation, but that's not always how it works. Spirits don't have vocal cords. They communicate through impressions, emotions, flashes of images, and shifts in energy. The trick is learning to translate what you receive into something usable.

The first step is training the mind to be still. If your

thoughts are chaotic, incoming transmissions get buried under the noise. Meditation isn't about silence; it's about learning to direct focus. When you can hold your attention without distraction, you create space for spirit voices to come through. This is why so many ancient magicians and mystics practiced stillness—it clears the way for reception. Start by sitting quietly and observing your own thoughts. If you can recognize your internal monologue, it becomes easier to notice when something foreign enters the mix.

Once the mind is still, the next step is learning to differentiate between imagination and genuine spirit contact. This is where many people struggle. The difference is in the texture of the experience. Your own thoughts are familiar, predictable. When a spirit communicates, it comes with a presence—an energy shift that feels external. It's the difference between remembering a conversation and having one in real-time. Pay attention to sensations in the body. Spirit communication often carries a weight, a tingling, or a sudden change in atmosphere. Some spirits project emotions before they send words, so a wave of sadness, warmth, or unease can be the first sign of connection.

Telepathy isn't just about hearing; it's about sensing. Some people receive messages as mental images. A spirit might not say "danger" but instead flash an image of a locked door or a crumbling bridge. Others get physical sensations—a tightening in the chest when a spirit is trying to warn them of something. The more you work with a particular entity, the easier it becomes to recognize their style of communication. This is why pathworking is so effective. By repeatedly working with a spirit, you establish a link, making their messages clearer over time.

One of the best ways to develop telepathic skills is through controlled exercises. Start by asking a question and clearing your mind for a response. If nothing happens, don't force it. Spirits don't communicate on demand like a radio station. Sometimes the answer comes later in a dream or as a thought that suddenly clicks into place hours after the ritual. The key is paying attention. The more you acknowledge subtle impressions, the stronger they become.

Spirit communication also improves when you use tools to bridge the gap. Pendulums, automatic writing, and scrying aren't crutches; they're training wheels. They help you bypass the analytical mind and receive messages in ways that are easier to interpret. Over time, as telepathy strengthens, these tools become less necessary. The connection stabilizes, and messages come through directly.

The last piece is trust. Doubt blocks reception. If you second-guess every impression, you'll dismiss real messages as imagination. Spirits won't waste energy forcing communication. They send what they need to, and if it's ignored, they move on. Confidence comes with practice. The more you work on telepathic reception, the clearer the messages get. Eventually, communication becomes natural—less like guessing and more like listening to a voice you've always known was there.

Intuition is the foundation of all magik. It's what lets you sense when a ritual is working, when a spirit is present, when something unseen has shifted in the energy around you. But intuition isn't a vague feeling—it's a skill, and like any skill, it can be trained. The subconscious already picks up on subtle details before the conscious mind processes them. The trick is learning to pull that hidden information to the surface and trust what it reveals.

The first step is recognizing that intuition is a form of pattern recognition. Your mind is always absorbing data, even when you aren't actively paying attention. A slight change in temperature, an unusual stillness in the air, a shift in the way candle flames move—these are all signs of something happening beneath the surface. The problem is that most people dismiss these impressions as random. Training intuition starts with stopping that habit. Instead of brushing off a sudden sense of unease or a pull in a certain direction, acknowledge it. Don't overanalyze—just note it. The more you pay attention, the more the subconscious starts pushing these signals forward.

One of the fastest ways to sharpen intuition is through exercises that engage the subconscious directly. Divination tools work well for this, not because they predict the future, but because they force you to interpret symbols and impressions without the interference of logic. Tarot, runes, or even a simple coin flip work by giving the subconscious an opening to communicate. The moment you stop thinking and just react to what the cards or symbols suggest, you're tapping into intuition. The more you do this, the stronger the instinctive responses become.

Another way to enhance this ability is to train the mind to recognize energetic shifts in real time. This means getting comfortable with sitting in silence and feeling the room before and after a ritual, noting the difference in how the air feels, how the space itself seems to change. Magicians who do this regularly develop a sensitivity to even the smallest disruptions. This is the level of awareness that allows you to detect when an entity enters a space before any physical confirmation occurs.

Dreams are another gateway to training intuition. The subconscious has no filters while dreaming, so messages come through clearly. Keeping a dream journal helps bridge the gap between waking and subconscious awareness. Over time, the connections between dream symbols and waking intuition become obvious. If certain images or sensations consistently precede real-world events, that's intuition sharpening itself through repetition. The subconscious is always a step ahead, but most people don't track its warnings closely enough to recognize patterns.

The final stage of training intuition is trust. The moment doubt creeps in, the connection weakens. The subconscious doesn't argue; it simply stops sending signals when ignored. This is why experienced magicians seem to "just know" when something is about to happen—it's not luck or superstition, it's trained instinct responding to signals most people overlook. The more you use it, the stronger it becomes. Eventually, you stop questioning and start knowing.

Using the Pendulum & Tarot

A pendulum and a tarot deck aren't just divination tools; they are amplifiers for ritual work. They act as extensions of the subconscious, tuning into unseen forces and pulling out the information buried beneath surface-level perception. When used correctly, they don't just predict outcomes—they sharpen focus, refine intent, and adjust energy flow to align rituals with the strongest possible current.

The pendulum is one of the simplest but most effective tools for direct communication with the energies at play. Unlike other divination methods, it responds immediately to shifts in the environment, making it ideal for checking the energy of a ritual space before casting. A pendulum can be used to confirm whether a spirit is present, if an altar is correctly charged, or if any lingering negativity needs to be cleared. It works because it bypasses conscious thought and reacts to the slightest energy fluctuations through micro-movements in the hand.

I think I've used a pendulum for at least 35 years, and I've incorporated it into magik for just as long. In many of my books, I recommend using a pendulum to listen to spirits.

The thing is, a pendulum can be tricky. You have to learn to let go of personal expectations. If you impose a desired answer onto it, you'll see exactly what you want to see—not what's actually there. The best results come when the mind is neutral, observing without interference.

I've seen pendulums react to wishful thinking and give completely wrong answers. Using one while anxious or rushed can also lead to inaccuracies, as the pendulum will reflect that unsettled energy rather than reveal the truth.

Tarot functions differently. While a pendulum answers direct questions, tarot unveils the deeper mechanics of a situation. Before a ritual, a reading can reveal unseen obstacles, the best planetary influences to tap into, or even which spirits are most aligned with the work. The cards provide a narrative—a symbolic reflection of what's happening beneath the surface. This is where interpretation matters. A single card drawn as a focal point for a ritual helps refine the intent, giving the subconscious something concrete to latch onto. It's not about the card having an inherent magikal property; it's about using it as an anchor, a visual link to the forces being called upon.

When used together, pendulum and tarot enhance ritual precision. The pendulum confirms whether the chosen timing is strong or weak, if the energy of a petition is properly aligned, or if an offering is sufficient. Tarot, on the other hand, maps out the best approach. It shows whether an adjustment needs to be made, whether something is being overlooked, or if a different spirit or method would yield better results. The balance between these two tools creates a feedback loop. The pendulum gives real-time responses, while tarot provides depth and strategy. This allows for dynamic, flexible ritual work where adjustments can be made before energy is wasted on something misaligned.

Some magicians take it further by incorporating these tools into the ritual itself. The pendulum can be used mid-ritual to verify when a spirit has arrived, while tarot can be drawn at the end to gauge the strength of the ritual's success. The key is treating them as active components, not just passive tools. They extend awareness beyond what the conscious mind can immediately grasp, ensuring that energy flows where it's needed with maximum efficiency. Mastering their use in ritual work creates a level of control that transforms basic spellcasting into something far more refined, deliberate, and powerful.

Detecting Energy Currents

Detecting energy currents is one of the most overlooked but crucial skills in magik. Most people focus on ritual mechanics—words, gestures, offerings—but if you can't feel the energy, you're operating blind. Energy is the raw force that drives everything in magik. You don't just push it; you have to sense where it already flows and align yourself with it. When you tune into these currents, your rituals shift from being

High Magik

mechanical processes to real interactions with unseen forces.

The first step is developing sensitivity. Energy currents aren't obvious at first, but they are there. If you've ever walked into a room and immediately felt tension, even before anyone spoke, you were picking up on energy. If you've ever stood in nature and suddenly felt lighter, more aware, that's energy too. The difference with magik is that you're training yourself to notice these shifts intentionally, not just when they hit you by accident. The easiest way to start is by working with your hands. Hold them a few inches apart and focus on the space between them. At first, it might feel like nothing, but if you stay with it, you'll start to sense a subtle resistance, like a magnetic push or a faint heat. That's energy. It's not coming from your hands; your hands are just tuning into it.

Once you recognize the feeling, the next step is expanding that awareness beyond your own energy. Every space has its own current. The moment you walk into a ritual area, stop and feel what's already there. Is it still, charged, chaotic? Before lighting a single candle, before casting a circle, take a moment to register what the space is doing naturally. If you're summoning a spirit, you should be able to feel the shift in pressure when it arrives. Some describe it as the air thickening, others as a static charge on the skin, or even a change in temperature. The key is to notice what shifts when you work magik. If you can't feel anything, you're either rushing through it or your mind is too distracted to register the change.

Energy doesn't just move—it flows. It has direction. When

casting a spell, pushing energy out is only part of the process. You have to feel where it's going. If the current resists, something is blocking it. If it feels weak, you're not generating enough force. If it scatters, you didn't focus it properly. A strong ritual will have a noticeable current, like standing in a river and feeling the water pulling around your legs. This is why some spells work instantly and others fizzle—when energy flows correctly, it carries intention like a current carries a boat. When it doesn't, it just disperses.

There's also the issue of natural energy currents, the ones that exist outside of your influence. The Earth has its own currents, and they don't always match what you're trying to do. Working against them is like trying to swim upstream. This is why timing and location matter. Some places amplify magik naturally, while others dampen it. If a ritual feels sluggish, the energy might not be moving because the space itself isn't conductive. You can override this by layering energy—using incense, candles, movement, or sound to build a charge—but if you're attuned enough, you'll know whether the space is naturally aligned with what you're doing.

Feeling the "flow" of magik in real time means being aware of feedback. If a spell is working, there will be a response. It might be a pull in your gut, a sudden change in the air, or an intuitive sense of completion. If nothing happens, something is wrong. This is where a lot of practitioners fail. They push energy out and assume that's enough. It's not. Energy moves in cycles. If you're doing a manifestation ritual, you should feel the energy return to you in some form. If it vanishes without a trace, the ritual was weak. If it rebounds too strongly, you might have built up too much force without properly directing it.

Magik isn't just about creating energy but also about reading it. If you train yourself to sense currents, you'll know when a ritual is finished without needing to check a clock. You'll feel when a spirit is still present, even if you don't see or hear anything. You'll know when a spell has taken root, because the energy will settle in a way that's unmistakable. Most people who struggle with magik aren't lacking power—they're lacking awareness. They aren't feeling what's actually happening. If you can detect energy in real time, you won't need to guess whether a ritual is working. You'll know, because the energy itself will tell you.

CHAPTER 9

Engineering Reality

My favorite part of magik is this—the ability to engineer "coincidences" and "synchronicities." Except in magik, there are **no** coincidences. Every outcome, every seemingly random event, is a result of intention and alignment. As someone with a science-minded approach, I see magik as a way to engineer reality itself, shaping it to conform to my will. This goes beyond simply practicing spells or rituals—it's about constructing a framework where manifestation is constant, structured, and reliable.

Magik is not just something we do; it's something we build. Like an architect designing a city, we don't just throw structures together randomly. We study the terrain, plan for energy flow, and create something that is both functional and powerful. This is what separates a magikal practitioner from a magikal architect. A practitioner casts a spell when they need something. A magikal architect designs reality so that their needs are already being met, consistently and effortlessly.

The first shift in thinking at this level is understanding that reality itself is structured, built on patterns of energy, thought, and interaction. Magik works because it taps into these existing structures, rearranging them to suit our desires. When we cast a spell, we are not creating something from nothing—we are adjusting the underlying blueprint of our existence. Every intention, every sigil, every ritual is a tool for shaping these patterns.

To truly step into the role of a magikal architect, we must stop thinking of magik as a reactionary tool—something to turn to when a problem arises—and start seeing it as a continuous process of reality engineering. This means proactive construction rather than reactive spellcasting. Instead of waiting until we need money to cast a wealth spell, we engineer a life where abundance flows naturally. Instead of working a one-time ritual for protection, we build an ongoing, reinforced system of shielding that operates at all times.

This shift in thinking also demands control over our personal energy and mental state. If we cannot control the structure of our own thoughts and emotions, how can we expect to control the structure of reality? This is why internal discipline is just as important as external ritual. A magikal architect does not allow chaotic thinking to interfere with carefully designed manifestations. Every thought, every emotional response, every intention is either reinforcing the reality we are building or disrupting it.

True magik doesn't just come from a single ritual, just as a building isn't created from a single brick. It comes from systems—layered, interconnected magikal structures that reinforce one another. A single protection spell is useful, but a well-designed network of protections—from personal wards to talismans to alliances with protective spirits—creates an impenetrable barrier. A one-time manifestation spell may bring temporary results, but constructing an ongoing manifestation system—a life that is energetically aligned with continuous abundance—creates lasting success.

This is where mastery of timelines and alternate possibilities becomes crucial. Manifestation is not about forcing something into existence—it is about aligning with the timeline where that reality already exists. Every possible outcome already exists in the vast web of existence. Our job is to lock onto the version of reality where our desires have already unfolded. This is why visualization, energy alignment, and becoming the person who already has what we seek are so important. Magik is not just about commanding the external world—it is about placing ourselves into the reality where our goal is inevitable.

This is also why precision is critical. When we build a structure—whether physical or energetic—every detail matters. If our energy is scattered, if our thoughts contradict our goals, if we introduce too much uncertainty, we create weak points in the structure. A magikal architect doesn't rely on vague desires; they craft clear, precise blueprints and execute them with focus and intention. They understand when to shape reality actively and when to allow it to unfold, balancing control with flow.

Spirits, rituals, sigils—these are tools, not the magik itself. The true work is in how we weave them together, how we construct reality from them. The more we refine our systems, the more seamless manifestation becomes. Instead of working magik in isolated moments, we reach a state where magik is embedded in our daily existence, running constantly like an unseen force shaping the world around us.

This is the true distinction: a practitioner works with magik. A magikal architect is magik. They see the patterns, shape the structures, and move through existence as a creator, not just a participant.

And once we fully embrace that role, reality itself bends in our favor—not just in moments of ritual, but in every moment of our lives.

Becoming The Creator

There's a point where a magician stops being just a magician and starts becoming something more—a creator of worlds. Most never make it past the first stage. They learn to cast spells, perform rituals, summon spirits, and work with energy, but they remain within the boundaries of the existing structure. They accept the world as it is and use magik to shift things within that world. That's a magician's approach—powerful, but still operating inside the framework of what already exists. A creator of worlds, on the other hand, rewrites the entire framework. They don't just bend reality; they design it.

Magicians work within the rules. They use the systems they've learned, channel energy, and make things happen, but they're still reacting to the world. They work with existing currents, adjusting what already is. A creator builds. They don't just manifest a specific outcome—they generate an entirely new reality, one where that outcome isn't an exception but a constant. Instead of influencing the present moment, they reshape the timeline itself, shifting to a version of existence where things unfold exactly as they will them to.

This is why most people stay magicians. It's easier to manipulate what's already there than to construct something new from nothing. Creation requires full control of thought, energy, and intention. It requires absolute certainty, not just in the magik being worked, but in the world itself conforming to the design set in motion. A creator doesn't hope for results. They don't even anticipate them. They live in the world where those results are already true. That shift in perspective is what makes the difference.

Most magicians make the mistake of seeing themselves as

separate from their magik. They work spells, call spirits, use sigils and symbols, but they don't see themselves as the source of the power. Even when they're highly skilled, there's still an underlying separation between "themselves" and "the magik they're working." A creator of worlds is the magik. There is no separation. Their very being shapes reality. Their thoughts ripple through existence. Their intentions become structure. When they speak, when they move, when they focus, they are actively crafting the world around them—not just through rituals, but through every action, every decision, every breath.

This is why reality shifts so easily for a creator. They don't need to fight against circumstances, because circumstances are born from them. A magician alters reality. A creator defines it. When they say something is, it becomes. Their magik doesn't have to break through resistance, because they never allow resistance to exist in the first place. A magician might work a spell for success and then wait for it to take effect. A creator exists in a world where success is already inevitable. The energy is entirely different. It's not a question of whether something will happen—it already has.

This level of creation requires a different kind of focus. Traditional magik involves directing energy, influencing probability, and working within the natural flow of things. Creating a world means controlling the flow itself. It means choosing what rules apply. It means refusing to acknowledge limitations. It means rejecting the idea that anything is "set" or "fixed" and instead seeing everything as malleable. People talk about "bending reality." A creator doesn't bend it—they write it from scratch.

One of the biggest shifts in thinking comes when you stop trying to work against reality and start seeing it as something that emerges from you. Most people treat reality like an external force, something they have to influence. A magician might push against reality to manifest a desire. A creator removes the gap entirely—there is no reality "out there" to struggle against. There is only what they are bringing into being.

This is why a creator doesn't just manifest small outcomes—they generate entire life patterns. Where a magician might use magik to find a new job, a creator reshapes their entire existence to be one where wealth, purpose, and opportunity naturally flow toward them. They don't just manifest love—they become someone who effortlessly attracts deep, powerful connections. Every aspect of life transforms, not just the pieces they focus on.

Time also functions differently for a creator. A magician thinks in terms of waiting for results, tracking outcomes, looking for signs. A creator does not wait. They do not check. They do not search for "proof" that their magik worked. Their certainty is so absolute that the timeline bends to match it. What they decide must happen—so it does. Not in a way that forces it, but in a way that is simply how things are. Their reality does not require confirmation. They do not question it, so it does not question them.

High Magik 303

This is why creators of worlds experience effortless manifestation. Not because they are more skilled, not because they cast better spells, but because they don't separate themselves from the result. They do not approach magik as something external to themselves. There is no gap between thought and reality. What they hold in their mind becomes what they walk through in the world. Their will is the law of their existence.

The real power here comes from understanding this isn't just about belief. A magician can believe in their spell and still fail. A creator does not acknowledge failure as a possibility. If something doesn't appear immediately, it's not because it didn't work—it's because the world is still catching up to their vision. They hold the structure steady, knowing reality will conform. They do not doubt, and because they do not doubt, there is no alternative but for their world to take form exactly as they willed it.

Moving from magician to creator means removing the last traces of uncertainty. It means understanding that you are not working with reality—you are designing it. Every word you speak, every thought you hold, every action you take is constructing the reality you walk through. Once this understanding is internalized, there is no need to struggle, no need to force. The world shapes itself around you.

Most people will never reach this level because it requires letting go of old ways of thinking completely. It means abandoning the idea that the world is something to change and embracing the fact that the world is something you generate from within. It means no longer thinking in terms of "working magik" and instead becoming the force that magik flows from.

A magician practices magik. A creator of worlds is the magik.

And once that shift happens, reality itself becomes something effortless—because you are no longer inside it. You are above it, outside it, crafting it from the highest level. And from that vantage point, anything is possible.

Limitless Manifestation

Stepping into limitless manifestation ability isn't about learning a new technique or discovering some hidden ritual. It's about shifting the way you exist. Most people think of manifestation as something they "do." They put energy into a spell, a ritual, a sigil, and expect something to happen in response. That's fine for ordinary magik. But if the goal is limitless manifestation, then there can't be a distinction between "doing" and "being." You don't work to manifest—you simply exist in a state where reality conforms to you.

To reach this level, the first thing to eliminate is effort. The more effort you put into manifestation, the more you reinforce the idea that what you want is separate from you. If you see it as something distant, something you must "reach for," then you're setting up a structure where it remains just out of reach. Instead of chasing after an outcome, you shift into the version of yourself that already has it. The goal is not to make something happen but to align with the reality where it already exists.

This is where most people get stuck. They treat manifestation as a linear process—first, they set the intention, then they do the work, then they wait for the results. That's a slow, clunky way of doing things. Limitless manifestation is instant. Not in the sense that a bag of money materializes in front of you the moment you think about it, but in the sense that the shift in reality has already begun before you even question it. The process is not "I want this, so I will manifest it." The process is "I have decided this is my reality, and now everything must move to match that decision."

This is why absolute certainty is the key. Certainty collapses all other possibilities. The second you doubt, you create space for an alternate reality where it doesn't happen. A mind that holds only one outcome gives the universe no other choice but to deliver. The moment you say, "It is done," and you believe it without hesitation, reality begins to move in ways that defy explanation. You don't check for signs. You don't second-guess. You don't even wonder when it will arrive because, in your world, it already has.

This isn't just about mental shifts. Your entire being has to match the frequency of what you desire. Every emotion, every thought, every action has to align. You cannot say, "I am wealthy" while reacting to your bank account with fear. You cannot say, "I am loved" while feeling unworthy. These contradictions fracture reality, making manifestation unstable. The energy you emit must be identical to the energy of the reality you are calling forth.

This is why identity is more powerful than individual manifestations. If you try to manifest a single event—money, a relationship, a job—it's like trying to force a puzzle piece into a picture where it doesn't belong. But if you become the person who already has all those things, the puzzle rearranges itself automatically. Reality is not resisting you—you are simply holding onto a version of yourself that does not match what you want. Change who you are, and reality has to shift around you.

This is also why time itself becomes irrelevant at this level. A person who still sees reality as linear will always be waiting. A person who knows their manifestation is inevitable no longer cares about "when" because they have already locked onto the reality where it exists. The universe arranges things in the fastest possible way—sometimes that means immediate results, sometimes that means setting things in motion in ways that don't seem obvious at first. But the timeline doesn't matter because the outcome is already guaranteed. When there is no impatience, no searching, no checking, results come effortlessly.

For limitless manifestation, you also have to eliminate resistance at the deepest levels. If there is any part of you that subconsciously doesn't want what you are manifesting, you will sabotage it. Most people carry hidden contradictions.

They say they want wealth, but deep down, they fear responsibility. They say they want love, but they are afraid of being vulnerable. These inner conflicts create distortions in the manifestation process. The fastest way to remove this is to examine every belief you hold and dismantle anything that contradicts your goal. You are not working to manifest something—you are removing everything that blocks it from naturally occurring.

This is why energy mastery is essential. If your mind is chaotic, your manifestations will be unstable. If your emotions are unbalanced, your reality will reflect that. This is also why most people struggle with manifestation—it's not that their magik isn't working, it's that their energy is inconsistent. They waver between confidence and doubt, excitement and fear, certainty and hesitation. Manifestation follows the dominant frequency. The reality that wins is the one you hold onto the strongest. If you lock onto a vision and never let it go, everything else falls away.

At this level, spirits, sigils, rituals—these are amplifiers, not necessities. You don't need them, but they can accelerate the process. A spirit can clear pathways, a sigil can reinforce energy, a ritual can solidify intent. But these are tools, not the source of power. The source is you. When you stop thinking of external forces as responsible for manifestation and fully accept that you are the creator of reality, everything speeds up.

There is no limit at this level because there is no concept of limitation left in your mind. The only reason most people struggle with manifestation is that they still believe in restrictions. If you think something is difficult, it will be. If you think it's impossible, it will be. The second you erase those limitations from your mind, they cease to exist in your reality.

Limitless manifestation is not about wanting anything. It is about being the force that reality bends to. When you reach this point, you no longer hope, wish, or even work for results. You command, and the universe obeys. Not out of force, but because it is simply the natural state of things. You are not separate from the process. You are the process.

The moment you fully accept that, nothing is beyond your reach.

CHAPTER 10

Contacting Any Spirit

On a daily basis, I get emails from readers who ask me to help them making contact with "X", be that spirit a deity or daemon, or other type of spirit. I always answer by letting the writer know that I'm not a spiritual telephone book (Magik Yellow Pages, back when people would consult a thick book which listed names and telephone numbers. Before the internet had google). I advise them to seek out social media boards (Reddit, etc) and ask there. Although, I do now offer a service where one can ask me about this, and I'll give a full answer, but, to paraphrase the late, great Harlan Ellison, ya gotta pay me for my time.

With my books and experimental magik, I will make initial

contact with any spirit only after consulting multiple texts, either in my library or online, which gives some information about that spirit. Being naturally psychic (*See Chapter 8*) I can usually think about a spirit and make initial contact. Full research on any specific spirit can take me days.

So, therefore, I can't just drop everything and do research on an obscure spirit for anyone who asks.

This is the purpose of this chapter.

I'll give you a rundown of my process.

Once I'm in psychic, telepathic contact with the spirit, I'll begin making notes and interview them, so to speak.

Sometimes, the spirit will reach out to you for contact. This happens quite often. In my group, I'll see posts about what to do if a spirit reaches out. If that is the case, work this chapter.

Spirits exist across many cultures, mythologies, and belief systems, each with their own nature, temperament, and purpose. Understanding their distinctions isn't about memorizing a rigid classification but about grasping their function, origins, and what they expect from those who seek them out. Gods, daemons, angels, ancestors, and lesser-known entities all have their own ways of interacting with humanity. Some require elaborate rituals, others respond to a simple call. Some guide, others test, and some exist entirely outside human concerns. Knowing the spirit you're working with—beyond just its name or a vague idea of what it represents—is foundational to spirit communication.

Gods are vast, ancient intelligences, tied to civilizations, myths, and sometimes the very forces of nature itself. They are not human, though they have been depicted in human form to make them more relatable. They function on a level beyond morality as we understand it. While some are benevolent, others are harsh, indifferent, or even destructive. Worship, devotion, and offerings have long been the means of interacting with gods. Some require nothing but recognition; others demand structured rites and unwavering faith. Their power is immense, but they are not always interested in individual humans unless that human makes themselves known through ritual, devotion, or sheer force of will. Gods do not necessarily need us, but some welcome our attention, and in turn, grant favors, insight, or raw power.

Daemons occupy a space between gods and mortals, often misunderstood due to historical shifts in language and perception. In ancient times, the word 'daemon' did not mean evil. It referred to spirits of knowledge, inspiration, or guidance. Many daemons are remnants of older gods, stripped of their former status and placed into a role that aligns more with personal influence than cosmic power. They can be fiercely independent, and many operate with a sense of strict exchange—you give, they give. They do not typically tolerate casual summoning. They expect respect, clear intent, and an understanding of what you are asking. If you approach them blindly, assuming they will operate like a generic spirit guide, you are likely to either be ignored or met with an energy that overwhelms you. They require a magician who understands both caution and confidence.

Angels are often perceived as messengers of divine will, but that definition barely scratches the surface of their true nature. They are vast, luminous beings with specific functions, often tied to the enforcement of divine order. They are not always comforting presences. Some are warriors, others are gatekeepers of knowledge. They respond to structure and authority, not mere pleading. Invoking an angel means stepping into a current of power that is immense, sometimes overwhelming. They have little patience for frivolous requests and are not inclined to waste their energy on anything that does not align with their purpose. If you seek an angel's assistance, be prepared for them to work in a way that serves the bigger picture, not just your immediate concerns. They rarely negotiate, and their presence tends to shift reality in ways that are undeniable but not always expected.

I don't work with angelic beings much anymore. I know their origins, and they're often an insufferable bunch. I find daemons much easier to work with.

Ancestors have a different relationship with those who call on them. They are tied to bloodlines, personal history, and sometimes the lands they lived upon. Unlike gods, they have lived as humans, so they understand the struggles of mortality. However, not all ancestors are kind, nor are they all interested in the affairs of the living. Some remain bound to their descendants out of duty or unfinished business, while others have moved on entirely. Ancestral veneration is powerful because it ties the practitioner to a direct lineage of energy, creating a bridge between past and present. It can bring protection, wisdom, or even direct intervention. But it also carries responsibility. If one's ancestors were deeply flawed or carried destructive patterns, those influences can also bleed into the practitioner's life. Knowing which ancestors to call upon—and which to leave undisturbed—is a skill that must be honed over time.

Beyond these well-known categories exist the lesser-known entities—spirits of place, forgotten deities, wandering intelligences that do not fit neatly into any system. Some of these spirits attach themselves to locations, feeding off the energy of the land or the emotions imprinted upon it. Some exist in hidden pockets of reality, only interacting with those who stumble upon them or seek them out with purpose. These spirits can be unpredictable. Some are helpful, some are tricksters, and others are neither. Working with them requires an intuitive approach, as many do not conform to traditional evocation methods. They reveal themselves when they choose, and often in ways that defy logic. The key to working with such spirits is respect and patience. Forcing interaction with an unknown entity can lead to unpredictable consequences.

Discernment is not just about identifying what kind of spirit you are dealing with but understanding whether you should engage with it at all. Not every spirit is meant to be worked with. Some operate on a frequency that clashes with human consciousness, leading to distortion rather than enlightenment. Others have their own agendas and may see the magician as a means to an end rather than an ally. Knowing the history, mythology, and true nature of a spirit is the first step, but experience, intuition, and careful observation are just as vital. If something feels wrong, it usually is. The best way to avoid trouble is to approach spirit work with clarity and confidence, not blind curiosity.

Responsibility in spirit communication is often overlooked in modern magik. Spirits are not vending machines for power or shortcuts to success. They are not obligated to assist simply because they have been called. Some spirits choose to help out of affinity, some out of mutual exchange, and others because they see potential in the magician. But a spirit will rarely continue working with someone who does not honor the exchange. Offerings, respect, and genuine engagement are necessary. If you approach spirit work with entitlement or desperation, you will either be ignored or drawn to something that feeds off your need. A practitioner must cultivate self-awareness, balance, and the ability to walk away when needed.

There is also the matter of what you are willing to give in return. Not all spirits require tangible offerings—some may ask for devotion, acts of service, or changes in behavior. Some ask for nothing at all, only recognition. Others will test your resolve, patience, or even your ability to handle power. If you are not ready for the responsibilities that come with spirit communication, then it is best to hold off until you are. Spirits can change lives, but they also reveal what is hidden within the practitioner. If there are weaknesses, unresolved fears, or doubts, those will be amplified. Spirit work is not for the hesitant or the unprepared.

Approach this path with respect, knowledge, and an understanding of what you are stepping into. Spirits existed long before us, and they will continue long after we are gone. They are not bound by human expectations, but they can teach, guide, and transform those who are willing to engage with them properly. Learning their nature, knowing when to call and when to remain silent, and understanding the balance of power between practitioner and spirit are the keys to meaningful spirit communication.

Researching Spirits

When researching spirits, the internet has become an invaluable tool, offering an unprecedented wealth of information. However, not all sources are equal, and careful discernment is necessary. Academic databases, such as JSTOR, Google Scholar, and university archives, provide access to peer-reviewed studies on mythology, anthropology, and religious traditions. These sources are essential for understanding the historical and cultural contexts of spirits, tracing their origins, and identifying variations in their worship and interactions with humans. Scholarly research gives a solid foundation, preventing misconceptions that arise from modern reinterpretations that often dilute or sensationalize the nature of these entities.

Beyond academic resources, the occult community has produced a vast network of forums, blogs, and books written by experienced practitioners. Websites such as The Digital Ambler, Rune Soup, and Hermetic Library house deep insights into practical magik, rituals, and direct encounters with spirits. Occult forums like the now-archived EvocationMagic or still-active Reddit communities such as r/occult provide firsthand experiences and shared methodologies. However, these platforms require discernment. Anecdotal evidence can be valuable, but it should always be cross-referenced with traditional sources and personal experience.

Digital libraries such as Sacred-Texts.com and the Internet Archive contain rare and historical grimoires, some of which were inaccessible until recently. These repositories offer direct access to primary sources, allowing practitioners to study translations of ancient texts rather than rely solely on modern interpretations. The Picatrix, The Key of Solomon, or The Grand Grimoire all have versions available in these archives, providing direct insight into older systems of working with spirits. When studying these materials, it's crucial to differentiate between historical rituals, which may have been designed for a different cultural or linguistic context, and adaptable methods that can be modified for modern practice.

Modern media has also become a key player in spirit

research. YouTube lectures, podcasts, and recorded discussions by well-respected occultists offer practical guidance and interpretations of ancient methods. Platforms such as Glitch Bottle Podcast, Rune Soup's interviews, and interviews with scholars like Dr. Justin Sledge provide useful commentary on grimoires, spirit traditions, and ritual techniques. While these sources are less rigid than academic studies, they often offer insights that bridge scholarly work and actual practice, making them an important part of a well-rounded approach.

While online resources are vast, real-world research is still irreplaceable. Libraries, particularly those in universities or specializing in religious studies, offer physical texts that may not be digitized. Folklore and anthropology sections often house collections of local myths, variations of well-known spirits, and firsthand accounts of spirit interactions recorded throughout history. Older books, especially those printed before the recent occult resurgence, often contain insights free from modern revisionist interpretations.

Historical grimoires found in special collections, museum archives, and private collections provide additional depth. Some of the most well-preserved texts are kept in academic institutions and require formal access requests. Museums dedicated to mythology, religion, or cultural artifacts also provide tangible connections to spirits through statues, tablets, and artifacts used in ancient rituals. Some of these institutions allow hands-on experience with these items, which can provide a powerful energetic link to the spirits they represent.

When I was a student, I was often found in one of the largest college libraries. I loved going through the shelves for obscure texts. Behind the counter and available by request were old books, many bound in the late 17th and 18th centuries. Most bound in animal leather, and I even was able to checkout an ancient grimoire which used actual parchment, the thin animal skin paper. Not that I was able to read it. I tried. (Is that an "f" or a funny "s"? Huh. No idea.)

Sacred sites and temples dedicated to specific spirits remain among the most potent research methods. Even if a spirit is no longer widely worshipped, the energy of these spaces often remains intact. Pilgrimages to such locations can offer direct communion with the entity in question, sometimes providing insights that no book or online source can offer. Whether it's an ancient temple, a shrine, or even a forgotten graveyard with local spirits, these places serve as focal points where the veil between worlds is naturally thinner.

For those seeking direct confirmation, personal divination is an essential step. Methods such as Tarot readings, the pendulum, and automatic writing provide feedback on whether a particular spirit is interested in communication. A well-formulated question, combined with an established divination practice, can reveal insights about a spirit's nature, temperament, and willingness to work with a practitioner. Tarot spreads designed to assess the intentions of a spirit can clarify whether it's beneficial to proceed. A pendulum, when used over a letterboard or sigil, can help confirm a spirit's presence or identity. Automatic writing, while more advanced, allows for direct communication, often bypassing mental interference if performed in a clear, meditative state.

Dreams and deep meditation offer additional layers of verification. Many spirits prefer to make first contact in the dream state, where the conscious mind is less resistant. Recording dreams immediately upon waking allows patterns and repeated symbols to emerge, indicating a spirit's attempt to communicate. Meditation, particularly when performed in a sacred space, can facilitate visionary experiences. Spirits often reveal themselves through persistent imagery, symbolic landscapes, or recurring thoughts that emerge seemingly from nowhere. By consistently engaging in these practices, a practitioner builds a reliable method for discerning genuine spirit contact from imagination or wishful thinking.

Combining all these research methods creates a well-rounded approach to spirit communication. Each has its strengths, and none should be used in isolation. Academic research provides historical context, online communities offer shared experiences, real-world exploration connects practitioners to spiritual energy, and divination provides direct feedback. The key is integration—using multiple sources to validate and refine understanding, ensuring that spirit work is rooted in both knowledge and experience.

Preparing for Contact

Preparing for contact with a spirit is not something that should be done haphazardly. It requires a structured approach, grounded in research and ritual. The first step is always to understand the nature of the entity being called. This is not just about reading the name of a spirit in a book and assuming that a single description is enough. Do not skip the research phase! This is crucial. It involves tracing the spirit's historical roots, identifying its functions, temperament, and past interactions with practitioners. This also includes understanding its cultural context—where it was originally venerated, how it was approached, and what kinds of offerings or rites were traditionally used. Spirits, much like people, respond better when approached with knowledge and respect rather than assumptions and demands.

Once the research is complete, the next step is setting up the space in a way that aligns with High Magik principles. This is not a casual calling; it requires the right atmosphere, tools, and focus. The space must be cleansed of disruptive energies, whether through incense, ritual purification, or a full banishing rite. The altar is prepared with intention, and every object placed upon it serves a purpose. Candles, chosen for their color correspondences, are placed accordingly. Incense is selected based on the preferences of the spirit, determined from historical records or prior experiences with similar entities. Offerings are gathered—these must be meaningful, tied to the spirit's nature, not simply chosen at random. Spirits recognize sincerity, and insincere gestures gain little traction in a serious ritual setting.

Invocation must be precise. High Magik does not rely on improvisation when it comes to first contact. Instead, it adheres to the structure and formal invocations passed down through grimoires and ritual texts. These are time-tested methods, refined through centuries of practice. Until a direct line of communication with the spirit is firmly established, it is best to use these traditional methods rather than attempting to impose personal techniques prematurely. This ensures that the summoning occurs within a known framework, one that provides stability and protection. Spirits, especially those of a higher order, respond to ritual structure. They recognize the energy and precision behind a well-executed invocation. A chaotic or poorly formed approach results in weak contact, miscommunication, or even the attraction of unintended entities.

Once initial contact is made, the nature of the working shifts. At this point, the practitioner's own magikal system becomes part of the process. Communication is opened, and from there, the spirit itself can guide the practitioner toward methods that are more attuned to their specific path. This is where the real work begins—establishing an ongoing relationship, refining the approach, and adapting the working methods to align with both the spirit's preferences and the practitioner's style. Some spirits will require formal settings for all future communications, while others will allow for more direct and personal interactions over time. But all of this must be earned. A structured foundation, rooted in respect and proper methodology, leads to a stronger connection, ensuring that future work is effective and aligned with the practitioner's path.

The first contact with a spirit requires focus, patience, and an understanding of how to attune yourself to non-physical energies. It is not a matter of simply speaking a name and expecting an immediate response. Spirits exist on a different vibrational plane, and your mind must be trained to perceive their presence. Before attempting contact, it is crucial to establish a state of calm awareness. Meditation is the most effective way to achieve this, as it quiets distractions and allows deeper perception to emerge. A simple method is to sit in a dimly lit space, free from external noise, and regulate your breath. The goal is not to empty the mind but to focus it, directing awareness toward the spirit's presence. The more refined your focus, the clearer the results.

A sigil or name mantra acts as a focal point to establish the connection. A sigil, crafted from the letters of the spirit's name or an established symbol linked to its identity, serves as a direct link between you and the entity. Fixating on the sigil while entering a light trance state deepens the connection, bridging the gap between the physical and spiritual. Some people prefer vocalization, using the name of the spirit as a repeated mantra. The resonance of your voice creates a vibrational key, gradually shifting consciousness into alignment with the spirit's frequency. If the spirit has traditional chants or invocations associated with it, these should be used, as they carry centuries of accumulated energy.

Visualization is another essential component. Once your breath is steady and the sigil or mantra has been engaged, turn your attention to building an image of the spirit's energy. This is not about forcing an image to appear but about allowing your mind to receive impressions naturally. Some spirits manifest as clear mental images, while others appear as colors, sensations, or symbolic patterns. Stay open to whatever form the spirit chooses. Often, subtle indicators begin to emerge—a shift in temperature, a flickering candle, an unexpected sound. These are signs that the veil is thinning and that the spirit is responding.

Establishing first contact is a process, not a single moment. The early stages require observation and interpretation. A response from a spirit may not be immediate or dramatic. It might come in the form of an intuitive nudge, a sudden thought that seems external to your own mind, or even a shift in emotional state. These subtle signs are just as valid as more overt manifestations. Testing the waters requires patience. If the spirit's energy feels heavy or resistant, it may not be the right time, or you may need to further purify the space. If there is a sense of warmth, a gentle pull, or a clear presence, the connection is forming. The more attuned you become to these subtle shifts; the easier future interactions will be.

I have had incense smoke begin to behave oddly, and then

I'd see shifting forms in the smoke. I've even photographed faces in the incense smoke.

Once an initial response is detected, the process shifts into deeper engagement. Acknowledge the spirit's presence, offer thanks for its attention, and make clear your reason for reaching out. This is a moment to listen, not demand. Spirits respond best to genuine respect and clarity of purpose. If communication is unclear at first, persistence and refinement of technique will improve results over time. First contact is a doorway. With practice, the connection strengthens, leading to clearer exchanges and a solidified relationship with the spirit.

Ritual for Spirit Communication

Prior to running this ritual, write a brief petition asking the spirit to establish communication and to work with you in the future.

Items Needed:
- Altar candles (two, preferably white or gold)
- Sigil or name of the spirit (drawn on parchment or carved into a candle)
- Incense (frankincense, myrrh, or one appropriate to the spirit)
- Offering (wine, honey, milk, or something relevant to the spirit)
- Offering vessel (small bowl or chalice)

- Ritual candle (color should correspond to the spirit's nature)
- Any other item representing the spirit (optional)

Ritual Steps:

Preparation of the Space:

Clear and cleanse the ritual area with incense or a banishing ritual. Arrange the altar with all necessary tools, ensuring the sigil or name of the spirit is placed centrally.

Casting the Circle:

Stand at the altar and visualize a sphere of light forming around you. Slowly turn clockwise, projecting energy outward, ensuring the space is fully contained.

Speak:

"I cast this circle as a bridge between worlds. Within this space, only truth and clarity shall enter. May it be sealed in balance and power."

Lighting the Candles and Incense:

Light the altar candles first, then the incense. Hold the ritual candle and focus your intent before lighting it.

Speak:

"By flame and smoke, I call forth the presence that seeks communion this night."

Meditation and Focus on the Spirit:

Take a few deep breaths, focusing on the sigil or spirit's name. Envision its presence, allowing any impressions to naturally arise. If using a name mantra or daemonic ENN, begin chanting in a steady rhythm, letting the vibration guide you deeper into the connection.

Invocation of the Spirit:

Read the petition aloud or recite an invocation specific to the spirit. A general invocation may be used:

"[Spirit's Name], I call to you across the veil. By your name and your nature, I invite your presence into this sacred space. Come forth in peace, in power, and in understanding."

Pause to sense any changes in energy—shifts in temperature, flickering candle flames, or an altered awareness.

Acknowledging the Spirit's Presence:

If the spirit's presence is felt, welcome it with respect:

"I honor your presence, and I seek your wisdom. If you are willing, reveal yourself in a way I may understand."

Wait and observe. If using a divination tool such as a pendulum, now is the time to employ it for communication.

Offering and Exchange:

Place the offering into the vessel, stating its intent:

"I offer this gift in gratitude and recognition. May our exchange be balanced and true."

Take note of any impressions, thoughts, or words that come to mind.

Closing and Farewell:

When ready to end the ritual, thank the spirit:

"[Spirit's Name], I thank you for your presence and guidance. May you depart in peace, as I close this space."

Extinguish the ritual candle first, then the incense. Close the circle by visualizing the energy retracting and dissolving.

Speak:

"This rite is ended. The connection is sealed. So it is."

Disposing of the Offering

Within 24 hours, take the offering to nature or leave it in a respectful place. Avoid keeping perishable offerings indoors for too long.

Recording the Experience

Write down everything noted during the ritual—sensations, messages, any unexpected occurrences. Tracking each ritual helps refine the approach and build a clearer connection over time.

This ritual establishes initial contact with a spirit through structured, High Magik methods. With repetition, the connection deepens, allowing for stronger communication and mutual understanding.

After completing the ritual and making initial contact with a spirit, the work is not finished. The next step is to evaluate the experience, understanding what occurred and determining whether further communication is warranted. This is where interpretation plays a crucial role. Signs may not always be immediate or obvious, and often, the spirit's presence lingers beyond the ritual itself. Energy shifts in the space, unusual synchronicities, vivid dreams, and even sudden changes in mood or perception can all be indicators that the spirit is still interacting on some level. Not all spirits communicate in direct words or images; many rely on subtler cues that require attunement to recognize.

One of the most common post-ritual occurrences is a shift in energy. This might manifest as a heavy atmosphere that lingers in the ritual space, an odd warmth or chill, or even an underlying sense of presence. Sometimes, objects in the area may seem slightly displaced, or candles and incense may have burned in unusual patterns. These are small but significant details. If a sense of peace or heightened awareness follows the ritual, it often indicates a successful connection. If the energy feels unsettled or chaotic, it may mean the spirit is not entirely receptive, or that something in the approach needs refinement. Tracking these shifts over multiple sessions allows patterns to emerge, making it easier to determine which spirits communicate most effectively and which methods yield the clearest results.

Dreams are another powerful means of post-ritual communication. Many spirits prefer to interact within the dreamscape, where the conscious mind is less obstructive and more receptive to their influence. After a ritual, paying close attention to dreams in the following nights is essential. A spirit may present itself through direct imagery, or it may use symbols that require decoding. An unfamiliar landscape, a repeated symbol, or even a conversation with a figure whose presence lingers upon waking can all be indications of continued contact. Keeping a journal to record these dreams as soon as they occur helps prevent the details from fading and allows for later analysis. Over time, the consistency of dream messages can reveal deeper insights into the spirit's nature and intent.

Beyond personal experience, synchronicities often act as validation. Encounters with specific names, symbols, or references in unexpected places can indicate that the spirit is acknowledging the connection. A symbol related to the spirit appearing randomly throughout the day, an animal traditionally associated with the entity crossing one's path, or an old book falling open to a relevant passage are all examples of this phenomenon. These moments should not be dismissed as mere coincidence. The more attuned one becomes to recognizing them, the more they serve as confirmation that the ritual succeeded and that the spirit is still engaging.

Journaling is an indispensable tool in spirit communication. Remember, write it all down. As discussed earlier, documenting every encounter, sensation, dream, or synchronicity as soon as possible is essential. Descriptions should include the emotions felt during and after the ritual, any environmental shifts, and any spontaneous thoughts or impressions that arose. Over time, this documentation builds a reliable record of interactions, making it easier to distinguish genuine communication from subconscious projection. Comparing entries across multiple sessions allows for patterns to emerge—whether the spirit tends to appear in a certain way, whether specific offerings strengthen the connection, or whether messages evolve in complexity. This process of recording and reviewing creates an evolving dialogue, ensuring that each interaction is understood in a broader context rather than as an isolated event.

The final step in evaluation is determining whether further contact is necessary. If the spirit's presence was strong and the communication was clear, ongoing engagement may be beneficial. However, not all spirits require frequent summoning. Some may only need to be called for specific guidance or at particular times of the year. Others may signal that their part in the work is complete. If interaction becomes strained, unclear, or consistently draining, it may indicate that adjustments need to be made—either in the approach or in the choice of spirit. Some spirits demand more structured offerings, while others require a more relaxed connection. If resistance is felt, reassessing the ritual methods or even the original intent of the summoning can provide clarity.

If a spirit does not respond at all, it does not always mean failure. Some spirits prefer to initiate contact on their own time. Others may not be compatible with the energy of the one calling them. If attempts at connection yield nothing, trying a different ritual format, cleansing the space more thoroughly, or even taking a step back for a period before reattempting may help. Forced interactions rarely yield meaningful results. Sometimes, the best approach is to trust that silence itself is an answer.

Evaluating a ritual experience requires patience and ongoing awareness. Every interaction, no matter how small, contributes to a larger understanding of how spirit communication works on a personal level. Some spirits will communicate readily, while others require persistence. The key is to approach the process as a relationship—one built over time, strengthened through experience, and refined through reflection. The more effort put into understanding the messages received, the more effective and transformative the practice becomes.

Troubleshooting

Sometimes, despite all preparations, a spirit simply does not respond. This can be frustrating, but it is rarely a sign of outright failure. There are many factors that could be influencing the outcome, and the key is to analyze and adjust rather than assume the connection is impossible. Spirits are not machines that respond on demand; they operate on their own terms, influenced by energy, timing, and intent. If the ritual has been performed correctly and no immediate response is felt, it is time to troubleshoot.

One of the most common reasons for a lack of response is an unclear or unfocused intention. The spirit needs to know exactly why it is being called. A vague request or a scattered mind can make the connection weak or inconsistent. Before the ritual, the purpose of the summoning should be refined. This does not mean a rigid script is necessary, but clarity in thought and expectation is crucial. If the desire is unclear to you, it will be even more difficult for a spirit to grasp. Taking time before the ritual to meditate on the exact reason for calling the spirit helps sharpen intent. If the request can be summarized in a few simple, precise sentences, it is usually strong enough.

Visualization is another key factor. Spirits do not exist on the physical plane the way humans do. Contacting them requires shifting awareness toward their frequency, which is why visualization techniques are essential. If the image of the spirit is weak or inconsistent in the mind's eye, the connection may not fully form. Strengthening visualization skills through dedicated practice can make a significant difference. This does not mean forcing an image to appear but rather allowing the mind to receive impressions clearly. Some people struggle with visualization but excel in other senses, such as feeling or hearing energy. Focusing on the method that feels most natural can help bridge the gap.

Timing can also be a crucial factor. Some spirits are more receptive at certain times, influenced by planetary alignments, lunar phases, or even the hour of the day. Spirits with solar associations tend to respond better during daylight hours, while those tied to the night or the underworld prefer darkness.

High Magik 303

If the first attempt fails, it may be useful to research the best time to try again. Lunar cycles, in particular, play a strong role in spirit communication. A waning moon is best for banishing or communication with the dead, while a waxing or full moon is more suited for making contact with guiding spirits or deities.

Energy levels also affect communication. If personal energy is low or erratic, the spirit may not be able to form a clear link. Strengthening personal energy through meditation, breathwork, or even physical movement before the ritual can help build the necessary force to sustain the connection. Grounding exercises ensure that energy is stable, while raising energy through chanting or drumming can amplify the call to the spirit. If the energy in the ritual space feels off, cleansing with incense or sound can reset the environment.

There are times when another spirit may be interfering with the process. Uninvited energies, whether benign or disruptive, can cause distortions in communication. If an unknown presence is felt or if sensations during the ritual feel different than expected, a quick banishing or clearing ritual should be performed before attempting contact again. Even the best-prepared spaces can attract unintended visitors, especially when working with open-ended summoning methods. A simple cleansing with salt, smoke, or a firm verbal command to dismiss any unwanted presence is often enough to resolve interference.

If direct summoning methods do not seem to work,

alternative techniques can be explored. A pendulum is a useful tool for checking if a spirit is present but unwilling to fully manifest. Holding a pendulum over the spirit's sigil and asking yes-or-no questions can provide confirmation of its presence. Pathworking is another effective way to establish contact when traditional methods fail. Instead of calling the spirit to a fixed location, this technique involves entering a deep meditative state and journeying to where the spirit resides. This method bypasses some of the barriers that can exist in structured rituals, allowing for a more fluid and direct experience.

It is important to recognize that not all spirits are immediately willing to engage. Some require persistence, others prefer to initiate contact on their own terms. If a spirit is entirely unresponsive, it may not be the right time, or it may not be the right spirit to work with. Forcing a connection is never advisable. If repeated attempts yield no results, stepping back and reassessing may provide a clearer answer. Sometimes, the silence itself is the message. Either the spirit does not wish to engage, or another spirit may be a better fit for the work being done.

Troubleshooting spirit communication is part of the process. Every attempt adds to the understanding of what works and what does not. Adjusting approach, refining techniques, and remaining patient ensures that, eventually, a breakthrough will happen. Spirits respond to sincerity, effort, and consistency. If the work is done with respect and dedication, the connection will come in its own time.

CHAPTER 11

Difficult Magik

I'm not saying that the following topics are totally impossible, but that the chances of success, or even modest success, is rather high. Making these topics somewhat difficult.

Yes, this magik does work.

It just may not work the way you want it to work.

This type of magik defies logic, a realm where the rules of probability seem to be rewritten, yet this magik is often dismissed outright as impossible. Not just by skeptics, but even by experienced magicians who've worked spell after spell with tangible results. This is the magik of what we call "the impossible"—working for outcomes that the rational mind would deem too far-fetched, too unlikely, or simply beyond the realm of what magik can accomplish. Yet, impossibility is a funny thing. What seems unattainable today can be mundane reality tomorrow. The problem isn't whether impossible magik works; it's whether we can control the conditions enough to make it work predictably.

The first barrier to working with difficult magik is the concept of probability. Probability is what determines whether an outcome is likely or unlikely. Magik bends probability, tilting the odds in our favor, sometimes so subtly we don't even realize how the shift happened. The vast majority of successful magik doesn't bring something entirely out of nowhere—it arranges circumstances so that what you desire becomes possible, then likely, then inevitable. Most of what magik accomplishes is just a forceful nudge, helping a possible outcome become reality. That's why love spells work best on someone already attracted to you, why money magik is more effective when it follows a job application or a business venture. There's a path for the energy to follow.

But difficult magik isn't working with slight probability shifts. It's going straight for outcomes that, to all appearances, have no logical way of happening. You want to heal an incurable disease. You want to manifest a lost artifact that vanished centuries ago. You want to completely rewrite your fate overnight. This kind of magik doesn't work by nudging probability—it's about breaking it entirely. And that's why it fails more often than not.

High Magik 303

The reason difficult magik fails so frequently is not because it's actually impossible, but because most people who attempt it do so with unrealistic expectations. They assume that if magik can manifest a hundred dollars out of nowhere, then it can also manifest a million. They believe that if a spirit can influence someone's thoughts, then it can make them love you unconditionally overnight. But the problem here isn't the scale of the magik—it's the force of reality resisting it. The bigger the shift, the more reality fights back. Difficult magik doesn't fail because it can't work, but because most people expect it to work like a simple spell, rather than an enormous restructuring of reality itself.

For difficult magik to succeed, it requires one of two things: a crack in reality where change is already happening, or a force powerful enough to override all resistance. This is why miracles tend to happen when everything is already in chaos—when someone is dying and suddenly recovers, when an impossible coincidence brings two people together in a way no logic could predict. When reality is already in flux, magik has a much easier time stepping in. This is also why difficult magik works best when channeled through divine or cosmic forces, not just personal willpower. A single person's energy isn't enough to force the universe into rewriting itself, but a god, an ancient force, or even an entire group of magicians focusing on one intent can sometimes create a shift powerful enough to make the impossible happen.

That's the paradox of difficult magik. It does work, just not in the ways we expect. A person who performs a ritual to erase all their financial problems might not wake up to find a million dollars in their account, but they may experience a bizarre chain of events that completely restructures their life—an unexpected inheritance, a sudden job offer, a chance meeting with someone who changes their career forever. Someone working a spell to cure a terminal illness might not see an instant recovery, but they may stumble upon an experimental treatment or an alternative method that somehow works against all odds. It's not that the magik fails—it's that it works along paths we don't see, using routes we never imagined.

This is also why patience is essential. Difficult magik rarely works instantly. It needs time to weave itself into reality, to create conditions where the improbable becomes inevitable. If you demand instant results, you will almost always be disappointed. This type of magik is like planting a tree—you don't expect to see it grow overnight, but one day, almost without noticing, you realize it has grown beyond what you thought possible. Those who succeed with difficult magik aren't just powerful magicians; they are patient, adaptable, and willing to work with the unexpected.

Set your expectations accordingly. Be prepared to "do the work" after finishing that money ritual. Use a "sweeting jar spell" to attract that lover.

As far as "chaos", I did a ritual to allow me to get back into the movie business, and that caused chaos in my life. Yes, I went back to Los Angeles, but it was really chaotic. I won't go into details, but this was a ritual to kali – and I was warned beforehand she will cause chaos, so I quickly got to the chaos (finding out) part quickly.

And yet, the biggest danger of difficult magik isn't failure—it's success. When you work with this level of power, there's always the risk that the outcome will be entirely different from what you envisioned. Manifesting an impossible amount of wealth might result in a sudden inheritance—but at the cost of a relative's life. A spell to change your life overnight might indeed do so—but in a way that forces you to let go of everything you once knew. Reality does not like to be rewritten, and when you push against it, it pushes back. The biggest lesson in difficult magik is to be very, very careful about what you ask for, because the results can be just as catastrophic as they are miraculous.

Ultimately, difficult magik is not for the beginner, nor for the faint of heart. It requires an understanding of how reality itself works, how probability bends, and how forces greater than ourselves interact with the world. It is the magik of those willing to take risks, to play with forces beyond their control, and to accept that sometimes, the price of success is far greater than expected. But for those who can master it, for those who understand the nature of probability and reality, difficult magik is the key to shaping the world in ways no one else believes possible.

Fast Money Magik – Why It "Doesn't Work"

There's no spell that can make a million dollars drop into your lap overnight, and yet that's exactly the kind of magik people want the most. Money magik is one of the most frequently requested forms of spellwork, and it's also the most misunderstood. Everyone wants fast money, usually because they're drowning in bills, desperate to escape debt, or just hoping for an easy way out. The problem is, money doesn't work like that. Unlike love, influence, or protection, money is purely a physical construct. It exists within systems, rules, and pathways, and unless those pathways are open, the energy has nowhere to go. That's why most fast money spells don't work—not because magik isn't real, but because people don't understand how to channel it properly.

At its core, money is a flow, not a thing. It isn't just paper or numbers in a bank account; it's an exchange of value. When you work money magik, you're not summoning a physical object—you're shifting the energy around wealth, clearing roadblocks, and opening doors that might have been closed. This is why spells for wealth tend to succeed when they create opportunities, but fail when they demand instant results. The moment someone expects cash to materialize out of nowhere, the spell is already set up to collapse.

Most fast money spells fail for one simple reason: they don't take physical reality into account. The most popular example is the lottery ritual. People assume that if magik can bend probability, then it should be able to manipulate the odds of a jackpot win. But the problem with this thinking is that the lottery is a massive system designed to be random. Millions of people are playing. The sheer weight of probability means that even if magik tilts the odds in your favor, the effect is microscopic. This is why even people who swear they've won on scratchers using magik never win life-changing amounts. At best, they walk away with a small prize. The system itself resists major shifts, and it takes more than a candle and a sigil to override the weight of millions of competing probabilities.

I have talked to magicians and I have seen proof that this difficult magik WILL get you a major win, but it's rare.

Another common belief is that money can't simply appear out of nowhere—but sometimes, it does. I once did a money spell and found a wallet on the street, no ID inside, just two hundred dollars in cash. That was real, and it was direct. The spell worked. It didn't summon money from the void, but it put me in the right place at the right time to receive it. This is how fast money magik can work—it bends reality just enough to create an opportunity that wouldn't have existed otherwise.

Sometimes, that means finding lost cash, like that wallet I found. Other times, it means stumbling upon an old check, getting an unexpected refund, or having a stranger hand you money for no apparent reason. These moments happen because magik shifts the flow, opening a crack where wealth can slip through. The mistake most people make is assuming this can be scaled up infinitely, that if a spell can bring two hundred dollars, it should also be able to bring two hundred thousand.

But reality doesn't work like that. It allows small shifts easily; bigger ones take far more effort, and usually a practical channel to work through.

This is also why wealth spells fail when they aren't paired with action. Magik is a catalyst—it speeds up what's already in motion. If nothing is moving, there's nothing to amplify. A person who casts a spell for financial success but refuses to look for new jobs, start a side hustle, or make any changes will see no results.

On the other hand, someone who works a ritual and immediately follows up with effort—networking, launching a business, or applying for promotions—will notice an almost supernatural streak of good luck. Suddenly, the right people appear, unexpected opportunities arise, and things fall into place with eerie precision. That's how real money magik works. It doesn't hand you wealth—it aligns you with it.

Despite all this, fast money magik does work under certain conditions. The key is understanding what kind of money can actually manifest. If there's already a source—a forgotten refund, an owed debt being repaid, a gift from a relative—then magik can accelerate its arrival. This is why money spells often result in unexpected checks, surprise bonuses, or even the sudden resolution of financial issues. The cash was already available, but the ritual removed whatever was blocking it.

Another way fast money magik works is by shifting opportunities instead of manifesting raw cash. Instead of money appearing, you get a job offer, a freelance gig, or a lucrative deal you weren't expecting. This frustrates a lot of people because they wanted instant wealth, not another job. But the reality is, most financial spells don't fail—they just don't work the way people want. A ritual for riches might get you a promotion. A spell for abundance might land you a business idea. These aren't failures. They're the exact mechanisms that allow wealth to enter your life. The problem is, most people don't want wealth. They want easy money.

The real test of money magik is what happens after the spell. If you do a ritual for financial success and immediately receive a job offer, the spell worked. If you asked for riches and suddenly find yourself with a chance to make real money, the magik is giving you exactly what you need. But most people reject these results because they require effort. They expect wealth to appear with no strings attached, so they ignore the opportunities right in front of them. This is why so many people believe their money spells failed, even when they didn't.

One of the most common examples of this is petitioning a spirit for riches and receiving an opportunity instead. Someone might call on a wealth daemon, ask for financial success, and then be offered a job that actually requires work. This feels like a letdown because they wanted the money, not the effort. But this is exactly how spirits operate. They don't drop cash in your lap. They open doors. The same thing happens with lottery spells—maybe you win, but it's only twenty dollars, not the jackpot. The spell didn't fail. It simply worked within the constraints of reality.

Ultimately, the reason fast money magik doesn't work for most people is because they misunderstand what it does. It's not about instant wealth. It's about removing resistance, increasing probability, and creating pathways for financial success. The moment someone lets go of the expectation that magik will erase all their problems without effort, they start to see real results. Fast money is possible—but only if you understand where it comes from.

Love Magik - the "Most Difficult"

Love magik is one of the most sought-after forms of magik, yet it is also one of the most prone to failure. When people approach love spells, they do so with intense emotions—desire, obsession, loneliness, heartbreak. These emotions can amplify the energy of a ritual, but they can also distort it, turning what was intended to be a simple attraction spell into something chaotic, obsessive, or outright destructive.

The core reason love magik often "doesn't work" comes down to free will interference. The universe, spirits, and the currents of magik itself are deeply tied to the concept of free will. (Free will isn't just an Earthly concept; our entire universe and reality revolve around it, regardless of how often it's violated on our planet.)

The moment you attempt to override someone else's

choices, the energy fights back. Many magicians learn this lesson the hard way. They cast a spell to make someone fall in love with them, only to find that the target suddenly becomes resistant, distant, or even repelled by their presence. The natural order has ways of balancing itself out, and love magik that seeks to manipulate tends to snap back.

Attraction and genuine connection are two entirely different things, and this is where a lot of practitioners go wrong. A binding spell does not create love. It creates entanglement, dependency, sometimes even obsession. People assume that if they can just get the person they want to stay close, then love will naturally grow. But forced attraction is nothing more than energetic pressure, and once that pressure lifts—either because the spell fades or because the person becomes resistant—the connection crumbles. Worse, a forced love spell can have long-term effects on the practitioner themselves. The energy of a manipulated relationship tends to linger, making future relationships difficult, messy, or entangled in karmic loops.

That being said, love magik can work under the right conditions. The key is shifting the focus from controlling another person to enhancing one's own aura of attraction. Instead of manipulating someone into loving them, a magician can work on increasing their own magnetism, drawing in people naturally. This form of love magik is much more effective because it aligns with the natural flow of energy rather than forcing a specific outcome. Love magik is at its best when it amplifies what is already present—strengthening an existing relationship, deepening bonds, or rekindling passion that has waned over time.

There is also a clear distinction between love magik and lust magik. Lust and passion are much easier to manifest than deep, long-term romance. Lust is a primal force, a raw energy that responds well to direct magikal influence. Spells to draw in sexual attraction, increase desire, or heighten physical connection tend to work because they align with natural biological impulses. But deep emotional connection? That's something built, not forced. Magik can assist in creating the right conditions for love to flourish, but it cannot fabricate love where none exists.

A classic example of ritual failure in love magik is when someone attempts to cast a spell on a person who has no romantic interest in them. The result is rarely love. More often than not, the target begins to feel uncomfortable around the practitioner, sensing something unnatural at play. In some cases, the spell turns into a feedback loop—rather than making the target obsessed, the magician becomes obsessed with the target, unable to let go of the desire they've amplified through their own work. This is why so many practitioners who focus on love spells end up trapped in cycles of longing, repeating the same spells over and over, never quite achieving what they want.

If love magik is to be successful, it must be approached with clarity and ethical awareness. Instead of bending someone's will, the magician should focus on shifting their own energy. This means working on self-love, confidence, and personal radiance. The most effective love spells are not about targeting a specific person but about making the practitioner irresistible to the right kind of partner. When energy is aligned in this way, the universe responds by bringing the right opportunities and people into the magician's life—without the backlash of karmic resistance.

Understanding why love magik fails is just as important as knowing how it succeeds. Many people fall into the trap of thinking that if their spell didn't work, they simply need to try again with more intensity. But love, unlike many other aspects of life, cannot be forced. It is fluid, changing, deeply tied to the free will of others. A wise magician recognizes this and works with the flow of attraction rather than against it.

Immortality

Immortality is one of the oldest obsessions in human history. The desire to extend life indefinitely, to halt aging, to exist eternally in the same body—these fantasies have driven countless myths, rituals, and experiments. From the alchemists' quest for the Philosopher's Stone to modern anti-aging research, people have always sought a way to defy time itself. But when it comes to magik, this kind of thinking often leads to dead ends. No matter how advanced a ritual may be, no matter how much energy is poured into it, the physical body is bound by limitations that no spell can fully overcome.

The problem is biological. The human body is not designed to last forever. Cells break down, DNA accumulates damage, and entropy takes its toll. The process of aging is written into the very structure of physical existence. Magik can influence biology—it can accelerate healing, increase vitality, even slow down certain aspects of aging—but it cannot completely override the fundamental laws of matter. The sheer energy required to keep reversing the aging process would be astronomical, constantly pulling against the natural cycles of life and death. Even if someone managed to stop aging temporarily, their body would still be subject to environmental damage, disease, and injury. Magik can extend life, but true physical immortality? That's an impossibility.

There's also the issue of stagnation. Many who attempt extreme longevity rituals without understanding the consequences end up encountering an entirely different problem: energetic burnout. The natural cycle of life includes growth, change, and eventual renewal. When someone attempts to halt that process entirely, they risk throwing themselves into a state where energy no longer flows properly. Their body may resist aging for a time, but the cost is often a kind of spiritual stagnation, a dulling of experience, a disconnect from the natural rhythms of existence. In extreme cases, practitioners have reported feeling "stuck," unable to move forward in any aspect of their lives, as if their very essence is trapped between worlds.

High Magik 303

But while true immortality is out of reach, longevity and preservation magik do work under the right conditions. There are countless rituals designed to promote health, slow aging, and extend life. These don't attempt to stop time but rather work with the body's natural regenerative processes, enhancing vitality and fortifying the spirit. Herbs, planetary alignments, energy work—these are all tools that can be used to maintain youthfulness and extend one's years. The difference is that these rituals align with the body's natural function rather than trying to force an unnatural state.

Another area where immortality magik does work is in soul preservation. The body may age and decay, but the soul is eternal. This is where a lot of misconceptions arise, especially regarding the idea of "selling" one's soul for immortality or power. The soul cannot be sold, given away, or taken. It is not a currency or a possession—it is the core essence of existence. Any deal that claims to offer immortality in exchange for a soul is a trick, a misunderstanding of what the soul actually is. What can happen is that someone can bind themselves to certain forces, entangle their energy in contracts that carry consequences, or even limit their own progression through misguided agreements. But the soul itself? Always intact, always returning to its source, always beyond any bargain.

There are techniques to ensure a form of continuity beyond physical death. Some traditions focus on soul transference—moving one's consciousness into another vessel, whether that be another body, an object, or an astral form. Others work with reincarnation magik, setting up conditions to ensure specific memories or traits carry over into future lives. These are forms of spiritual immortality, ways to extend influence or awareness beyond a single lifetime. But they are not physical immortality. The body will still age. It will still break down. The key is understanding that true survival is not about resisting change but about mastering continuity.

Ritual failures in this area tend to be dramatic. One of the most common is the attempt to "never age," a direct spell designed to freeze time on a biological level. These spells often backfire, leading to energetic stagnation or even accelerating the aging process instead. The practitioner may find themselves feeling drained, exhausted, or disconnected from life itself. Others may experience a kind of energetic paralysis, where nothing in their lives seems to move forward—no new opportunities, no personal growth, no real sense of progress. This happens because time is not just a force acting on the body; it is a flow that runs through all aspects of existence. Trying to halt it completely is like damming a river without considering the flood that will follow.

The smarter approach is to work within the boundaries of what is possible. Strengthening life force, preserving vitality, ensuring spiritual continuity—these are all forms of immortality that actually work. Instead of battling time, the goal is to align with the best possible version of one's existence, maintaining energy, health, and awareness for as long as possible. Aging can be slowed, life can be extended, and the soul will always endure. But the dream of endless physical life? That remains impossible, and for good reason.

Defying Reality

Magik is powerful, but it has limits. One of the biggest misconceptions people have when they start working with magik is the belief that they can override the fundamental structure of reality itself. Flying, teleportation, superhuman strength—these ideas show up in mythology, fantasy, and pop culture, fueling the belief that with the right spell or enough energy, anything is possible. But magik doesn't work that way. The physical world has rules, and while magik can bend them in subtle ways, it cannot fully break them.

The problem with attempting extreme reality-defying magik is that the physical body is bound by natural forces. Gravity, inertia, the density of matter—these are not just arbitrary rules that can be rewritten by will alone. A human body cannot suddenly generate the lift required to defy gravity. Muscles do not magically gain the strength to launch someone into the air or allow them to pass through solid objects. The energy required to break these physical laws is far beyond what the human system can generate, no matter how much focus or ritual work is involved.

That being said, not all aspects of these desires are completely impossible. Magik does work through perception, altered states, and subtle shifts in the way energy interacts with the world. Astral travel, for example, is a legitimate way of experiencing "teleportation." While the physical body remains grounded, the consciousness can travel anywhere, unbound by space and time. This form of movement is commonly mistaken for actual teleportation when, in reality, it is the projection of awareness to another place. Many who practice astral travel report experiences so vivid that they feel as if they were physically present somewhere else, but this is a mental and energetic experience, not a literal physical relocation.

Similarly, enhancing physical abilities through mental mastery is a real, functional aspect of magik. There are countless stories of monks, warriors, and advanced practitioners of energy work who seem to defy normal human limitations—enduring extreme temperatures, moving with seemingly impossible speed, demonstrating feats of endurance that science struggles to explain. These are not superpowers in the traditional sense, but they are evidence that the mind has a far greater influence over the body than most people realize. Through rigorous training, meditation, and focused energy work, it is possible to amplify physical abilities beyond what is considered normal. But this is refinement, not defiance. The limits of biology still apply.

Perception shifting is another area where magik can create what appears to be an impossible effect. Many spells for invisibility, for instance, do not make the practitioner physically vanish. Instead, they alter the way others perceive them. Someone working an invisibility spell may find that people simply don't notice them, that they blend into the background, that their presence doesn't register in a way that draws attention. This is a shift in awareness, not a literal vanishing act. The same principle applies to other forms of transformation—rather than changing the actual body, the magician changes how they are perceived, how energy moves around them, how their presence interacts with the world.

Ritual failures in this area tend to come from misunderstanding how magik functions. A common example is someone performing a ritual to become invisible, expecting to disappear entirely. What often happens instead is that they start feeling unseen in ways they didn't intend—people ignore them, opportunities slip by, their presence seems diminished rather than hidden. This is because the magik worked on an energetic and psychological level, not a physical one. The practitioner, in essence, told the universe, "I want to be unseen," and the universe responded by making them unnoticed in social and energetic ways, not by bending the laws of light and matter.

While reality itself cannot be completely rewritten, it can be influenced. Magik is about working with the subtle, the unseen, the possible. The real power lies not in trying to defy the laws of physics but in learning how to move through reality with greater awareness, control, and mastery. Those who understand this are the ones who see results, while those who chase the impossible often end up frustrated, burned out, or disillusioned.

Making the Impossible Possible

Magik isn't about making the impossible happen—it's about understanding how reality works and then shifting it in your favor. The biggest reason magik fails is that people approach it with an unrealistic mindset. They want to leap over every limitation without understanding how those limitations actually function. They try to force changes without first laying the foundation for those changes to occur. This is why so many beginner magicians struggle with results. They assume magik should work like a miracle, bending the world to their will with a single spell, but that's not how the system operates.

The key to making the impossible possible is shifting perspective. If magik isn't working, it's not because magik itself is weak—it's because the approach is flawed. Instead of trying to break the rules of reality, the smarter move is learning how to work within them. This doesn't mean settling for less. It means understanding how energy flows, how probability works, and how to align with forces that actually support manifestation. The more a practitioner learns to see the structure of reality as something flexible rather than rigid, the more effective their magik becomes.

One of the most common examples of misguided magik is the obsession with winning the lottery. People assume that if they pour enough energy into a spell, they should be able to make the universe deliver them a jackpot. But the problem here isn't that money magik doesn't work—it's that the method being used is wildly inefficient. The odds of winning the lottery are astronomically small. Trying to manifest something so improbable is a waste of energy. The smarter approach is to work with magik in a way that actually aligns with existing probabilities. Instead of demanding an impossible win, a magician should use wealth magik to create opportunities for financial growth, open pathways to abundance, and tilt circumstances in their favor.

Magik doesn't just drop money from the sky, but it does have a way of putting the right people, ideas, and chances in front of those who know how to work with it. It's the difference between forcing something to happen versus making yourself a magnet for wealth. Those who learn to work magik properly don't need to rely on something as unstable as a lottery win because they create multiple pathways for wealth to flow to them. The money appears, but in ways that are sustainable and natural.

Love magik follows the same principle. People fail when they try to force love onto a specific person, but they succeed when they turn the energy inward and make themselves irresistible. Attraction is an energetic force, not just a physical one. Someone who radiates the right energy naturally draws in the type of connections they desire. Magik amplifies this effect by fine-tuning the aura, shifting the way others perceive and react to the practitioner. A properly executed love spell isn't about bending another's will—it's about amplifying personal magnetism to the point where the right people are drawn in effortlessly.

The same logic applies to luck. There's no such thing as a universal force of good or bad luck. What people call luck is really just a mix of perception, mindset, and the removal of blockages. When someone feels unlucky, it's often because they're operating under unseen restrictions—mental patterns, external energies, or even subconscious sabotage. Magik works not by changing luck itself but by clearing away the obstacles that prevent good outcomes. It shifts the probabilities in a way that allows success to come more easily.

This is the real secret to making magik work: it functions within the framework of reality. Instead of trying to force things that are statistically or physically improbable, a magician learns to work with what's already possible and then expand upon it. Once this realization clicks, everything changes. Magik becomes fluid, responsive, and highly effective. It stops being about struggle and starts being about alignment. Those who master this understanding don't waste time on impossible goals—they reshape their reality in ways that make success inevitable.

CHAPTER 12

Oils and Powders

Yes, you can purchase very powerful oils and powders. These items are available in any reputable magik store, and online. I know of a witch who can make the best powders and oils; she throws her entire being into making these, and they're very effective.

We'll begin with the oils.

The Power of Oils

Oils serve as a bridge between the material and the energetic, allowing intention to be infused into physical objects while also acting as a carrier for spiritual power. These oils, whether formulated from essential oils, herbs, or resins, have been used across centuries and traditions to draw in specific influences, set the tone for ritual, and enhance the effectiveness of magik. What makes oils particularly effective is their ability to hold onto energy. They absorb intent, allowing the magician to work with them as an extension of their will, embedding their desire into a tangible form that lingers long after a ritual is complete.

Using oils in magikal work isn't just about adding a nice scent to the space. These oils, when properly prepared, can amplify energy, solidify an intention, or act as a direct offering to a spirit. The act of applying oil to an object, whether it be a candle, a piece of parchment, or even the skin, is itself a magikal act—a deliberate moment where energy is transferred, fixed, and directed toward a goal. When anointing something with oil, it isn't just a surface-level application. The oil seeps into the material, creating a lasting imprint. This is why oils have been favored for candle dressing, sigil work, and even as a substitute for incense when burning herbs isn't an option. They work by binding the intent to the object, making the physical item an active participant in the working, not just a tool.

Candle magik is one of the most obvious uses for magikal oils, and it's also one of the most effective. A properly dressed candle becomes more than just wax and wick—it turns into a vessel that holds and releases energy in a controlled manner. The choice of oil depends on the nature of the working, and the way the oil is applied matters. Some traditions dictate that oil should be rubbed in one direction to draw something in, while in another direction to repel. This kind of detail becomes significant in spellwork, where every action reinforces the intent. A money candle anointed from the base upward pulls wealth in, while a banishing candle rubbed from the top down sends unwanted energy away. The oil doesn't just prepare the candle for the working; it becomes part of the magikal equation itself.

Beyond candles, oils are used to anoint and charge objects. Ritual tools, statues, amulets, and sigils can all be enhanced by oil, each application strengthening the link between the object and the energy it is meant to carry. This practice is particularly useful when working with spirits, as many deities and entities respond well to scent-based offerings. Some spirits even have specific oil preferences, making this a direct method of establishing rapport. Anointing a sigil with an appropriate oil not only activates it but can also serve as a method of sealing a pact with a spirit or reinforcing an intention over time. In many cases, once the oil is applied, the object retains that specific energetic charge, becoming a standing link to the working.

Another direct use of magikal oils is through personal application—anointing the body to shift energy, strengthen aura, or align with a particular working. Some oils are meant to be worn to enhance attraction, open psychic channels, or shield against negativity. In this case, placement matters. Oils dabbed onto pulse points, such as the wrists, temples, or behind the ears, allow the body's natural heat to disperse the scent and energy more effectively. Some oils work best when placed on the third eye, palms, or the soles of the feet, depending on the intent. An oil meant to boost confidence might be applied to the throat or solar plexus, while one used for protection might be placed along the base of the skull or the edges of the aura itself. This practice can turn something as simple as applying oil into a daily act of magik, reinforcing intention without the need for a full ritual.

For those who cannot burn incense due to environmental restrictions, magikal oils provide an excellent alternative. Essential oils, when diffused into the air, can create the same energetic effect as burning corresponding herbs. A few drops placed in a diffuser or on a warm surface can shift the energy of a space in much the same way as smoke. When incense is traditionally used to call a spirit, oil can be placed on a candle or anointed onto the petition paper instead, offering the same connection in a more subtle way.

Magikal oils, once prepared, hold onto energy and intention for long periods, making them an invaluable tool for both immediate and long-term workings. The longer they sit with an intent infused into them, the stronger they become. Unlike other ritual components that dissipate or are consumed during the working, oils remain active, their power building over time. A bottle of properly crafted oil can last for years, growing more potent with each use.

Understanding the role of oils in magik is essential for any practitioner looking to refine their workings. The key is in their ability to hold onto energy and extend the reach of a ritual beyond the immediate moment of its casting. Whether used on candles, tools, sigils, or the body, the right oil can magnify an intention, creating a lasting effect that continues working long after the initial ritual is complete.

The Power in Magik Powders

Magik powders are one of the most direct ways to work energy into the physical world. Unlike oils, which absorb and hold onto energy through liquid, powders disperse it, scattering influence wherever they are placed. They move energy outward, influencing the space, objects, or people they come into contact with. This makes them especially effective for work that requires spreading intent over a wide area or setting energy into motion. Powders are used to coat candles, dust onto objects, sprinkle in specific locations, or even dress the skin. Some are meant to attract, some to repel. Some stay where they are placed, working quietly over time, while others rely on movement, riding the wind or foot traffic to spread their effect.

Because powders integrate so easily into daily life, they are an excellent way to work magik subtly. Once prepared, they hold energy indefinitely, making them easy to store and use as needed. A properly crafted powder doesn't lose potency over time; if anything, it becomes stronger, especially if it's repeatedly charged with the same intent. The blend itself determines its use. Some powders focus on attraction, drawing in love, money, influence, or luck. Others act as warding agents, protecting a space from intrusion or driving unwanted forces away. There are powders meant to break down obstacles, confuse enemies, or even stir chaos when necessary.

When used for candle magik, powders amplify the energy of the working, binding intention into the wax. A candle that has been anointed with oil and then dusted with powder becomes a layered magikal tool. The oil holds onto the intention, while the powder works as an activator, dispersing the energy as the candle burns. The type of powder used depends on the working. A prosperity candle might be coated in a blend of herbs and minerals aligned with wealth, while a protection candle could be dusted with something sharp, bitter, or fiery to create a barrier. Even without oils, powders can be pressed directly into the surface of soft wax or sprinkled around the base of a candle, setting up an energetic field that reinforces the spell's intent.

Powders can also be applied to objects to charge or repurpose them for magik. Ritual tools, sigils, personal belongings—anything can be dusted with a magikal powder to alter its energetic charge. A sigil sprinkled with an attraction powder will work more aggressively toward its goal, while a protective charm dusted with a defensive blend will hold stronger against outside interference. Some practitioners use powders to mark boundaries, creating protective or commanding lines around altars, doors, or ritual circles. In this way, powders function similarly to physical warding techniques, setting a defined energetic perimeter.

One of the more traditional uses of magik powders is through direct application to the skin. Some powders are designed to be worn, enhancing personal energy, boosting confidence, or attracting attention. A well-made powder can be lightly dusted onto the hands before a business transaction, pressed into the pulse points to enhance charisma, or even worked into the hair and clothing for long-lasting influence. These powders aren't just about scent or texture; they are charged materials, infused with intent and designed to shift how others perceive and react to the wearer. The energy they carry extends beyond the physical, creating an aura that subtly manipulates the environment.

For workings that require stealth, powders offer a powerful advantage. Unlike candles, which must be burned, or oils, which need to be applied with care, powders can be left behind without drawing attention. A well-placed powder can affect a space long after it has been scattered, influencing anyone who comes into contact with it. Some powders are meant to be stepped on, set in doorways or pathways where their energy will cling to the target. Others work by resting in a space, slowly altering the energy around them. A powder dusted onto a chair, a doorknob, or even mixed into soil can create subtle but lasting changes.

The method of dispersal plays a key role in how powders

work. Some are thrown to the wind, meant to carry an intention across distance, while others are sprinkled in controlled patterns to direct their effect. Powders laid in a straight line form a barrier—crossing them means stepping into the working's influence. A circle of powder can create a contained space of power, amplifying energy within it while keeping outside forces at bay. In this way, powders are often used to reinforce spellwork, creating physical links between the spell and the environment.

Because of their versatility, powders are one of the most adaptive magikal tools available. They require no flame, no liquid, no extended ritual setup—just a firm intention and a place to work. They can be blended in small or large batches, stored indefinitely, and used on the spot whenever needed. A single bottle of a well-crafted powder can serve dozens of workings, adapting to different situations without losing potency. Whether they are used in candle magik, personal anointing, object charging, or environmental manipulation, powders offer a direct, efficient way to extend influence and manifest intent in the physical world.

Recipes
How to Make a Magikal Oil

The base of most magikal oils is a carrier oil, such as almond oil, olive oil, or fractionated coconut oil. Essential oils and herbs are then added based on their correspondences.

Simple Money Drawing Oil

¼ cup carrier oil (almond or olive oil)

5 drops sandalwood oil

5 drops patchouli oil

2 drops ginger oil

2 drops vetiver oil

1 drop orange oil

Mix all ingredients in a small bottle and shake gently. Let it sit for at least 24 hours before use. Anoint candles, paper money, or doorways to attract financial abundance.

Love & Passion Oil

¼ cup carrier oil

2 drops rose geranium oil

2 drops ylang-ylang oil

1 drop cinnamon oil

1 drop vanilla extract

A pinch of dried rose petals

Let the mixture rest for a week, shaking it gently each day. Use to anoint love candles, sigils, or even pulse points to draw in romance.

Road Opener Oil (Unblocking & Clearing)

¼ cup carrier oil

5 drops lemongrass oil

3 drops orange oil

2 drops peppermint oil

Dried abre camino leaves

A small piece of High John root

This oil is great for clearing away obstacles. Use it on yellow or orange candles for best results.

How to Make a Magikal Powder

The base of a powder is usually finely ground herbs, flowers, resins, or roots. A mortar and pestle or a coffee grinder can be used to blend everything together.

<u>Attraction Powder</u>

Dried rose petals

Cinnamon powder

Ground nutmeg

A pinch of sugar

Use this powder to attract love, money, or positive energy. Sprinkle around candles, your altar, or even in your shoes before going out.

<u>Banishing Powder</u>

Crushed black salt

Dried sage

Dried rosemary

Red pepper flakes

Best for clearing negative energy. Sprinkle in doorways or burn with charcoal.

<u>Success & Confidence Powder</u>

High Magik 303

Ground cinnamon

Dried bay leaves

Lemon zest (dried and ground)

Crushed frankincense resin

Dust onto candles or sigils for a boost in confidence and career success.

Recipe for Hotfoot Powder

Cayenne Pepper (or red pepper flakes) – Creates agitation, irritation, and urgency to leave.

Black Pepper – Adds an aggressive push, increasing conflict and discomfort.

Sulfur Powder – Breaks ties and disrupts stability, ensuring the target cannot settle or return.

Graveyard Dirt – (Optional) Strengthens the powder's force by calling in ancestral or restless spirits to push the person out.

Crushed Red Brick Dust – Forms an energetic barrier, making return impossible.

Salt or Black Salt – Cleanses the area after the person has left, sealing it off from their energy.

All ingredients should be finely ground into a consistent powder. The stronger the ingredients, the more powerful the result. Some practitioners like to charge the powder under a waning moon or with a personal curse spoken over it, setting the full intention that the target will leave and never return.

(Place a small amount where your target walks, preferable

on their doorstep. Or, sneak it into their shoes. The idea is that the powder clings to them, embedding its energy into their life until they are forced to leave. If laying it in a direct path isn't an option, it can be dusted onto objects they frequently touch, mixed with dirt in areas they frequent, or even thrown into moving water while calling for their departure.)

Glossary of Terms

A

Akashic

The *Akashic Records* are a metaphysical repository containing all knowledge of past, present, and future events. They exist on a higher spiritual plane and can be accessed through deep meditation, astral travel, or advanced psychic techniques. Magicians seek the Akashic Records for wisdom, hidden truths, and guidance on their personal magikal paths.

Alpha State

A mental state associated with relaxation, light meditation, and enhanced creativity. It occurs when brainwaves slow to the alpha frequency (8–12 Hz), making it easier for magicians to enter trance states, strengthen visualization skills, and prepare for deeper magikal work, such as spirit communication or energy manipulation.

Altar

A sacred space designated for ritual work, usually a physical table or surface where ritual tools, candles, offerings, and sigils are arranged. The altar acts as a focal point for magikal energy, helping to amplify intention and facilitate interaction with spirits or deities.

Anchor (Astral Projection)

A technique used to facilitate out-of-body experiences. Instead of forcing separation from the body, the magician shifts their awareness to an external point (such as a spot on the ceiling or a floating energy signature). This method reduces resistance and allows for smoother transitions into the astral plane.

Anoint

A sacred act of applying ritual oils, perfumes, or consecrated liquids to objects, people, or spaces. Anointing is often performed to bless, empower, or sanctify items such as candles, sigils, and even the magician themselves before a ritual.

Aphrodite

The Greek goddess of love, beauty, desire, and passion. She is sometimes invoked in love magik, attraction spells, and rituals designed to enhance personal magnetism, sensuality, and romantic influence.

Apollo

A Greek god associated with the sun, prophecy, healing, music, and intellectual pursuits. In high magik, Apollo is called upon for clarity, foresight, artistic inspiration, and strengthening divination practices.

Astral

A term referring to the *astral plane*, a non-physical realm where spirits, thought-forms, and consciousness interact beyond physical reality. It is accessible through astral projection, lucid dreaming, and deep meditative states.

Astral Temple

A personal, self-created structure in the astral plane, designed by the magician as a sacred working space. An astral temple can function as a place of ritual, a knowledge repository, or a power source for storing and amplifying magikal energy.

Astral Travel

The act of projecting one's consciousness beyond the physical body to explore different planes of existence. It is a core skill in high magik, allowing practitioners to visit spiritual dimensions, communicate with entities, and access hidden knowledge.

Attunement

A process by which a magician aligns their energy with a specific force, deity, or current of power. This can be done through meditation, ritual practice, or focused intention, allowing for deeper spiritual connections and increased magikal effectiveness.

B

Binding

A type of spell or ritual designed to limit, restrict, or control the actions of a spirit, entity, or individual. Binding magik is often used for protection, preventing malevolent forces from causing harm, or securing an entity to a specific task.

C

Channeling

A practice where the magician allows messages, energy, or guidance from spirits, deities, or higher intelligences to flow through them. Channeling can take various forms, including automatic writing, vocal speech, or direct impressions received through trance states.

Circle Casting

A ritual technique used to create a protective boundary around a sacred space. The circle acts as a barrier that keeps unwanted energies out and enhances the power of the working within it. Magicians often cast circles before summoning spirits, invoking deities, or working major spells.

D

Daemon

A term referring to a type of spirit, often misunderstood as inherently malevolent. In high magik, daemons are powerful non-physical entities that can be allies or teachers if approached with respect and proper ritual protocols.

Detachment

A crucial mindset in magik that involves letting go of emotional fixation on an outcome. Detachment ensures that energy flows freely, allowing a ritual to work without interference from doubt, fear, or obsession over results.

E

Egregore

A collective thought-form or energetic construct created by a group's shared focus and intent. Egregores develop over time, gaining semi-autonomous power. They are commonly found in magical orders, religious practices, and long-term group workings.

Evocation

The act of summoning a spirit, deity, or non-physical entity into a defined space. Unlike invocation (which draws the entity into the magician's body), evocation calls the entity forth to appear externally and interact on its own terms.

H

High Magik

A term referring to structured and ceremonial magikal practices that involve advanced techniques, ritual invocations, and interactions with higher spiritual forces. It contrasts with low magik, which focuses on practical spellcasting for everyday needs.

I

Invocation

A ritual act of calling a spirit, deity, or energy into the magician's presence or even into their own body. Invocation is used to merge energies and temporarily embody a higher power's qualities or wisdom.

P

Pathworking

A visualization-based technique used to explore spiritual realms, make contact with entities, or receive guidance from higher forces. It often involves guided journeys through symbolic landscapes that represent deeper levels of consciousness.

Planetary Magik

A system of magik that aligns rituals and spells with celestial influences. By working with planetary hours, sigils, and correspondences, a magician can enhance spells for wealth (Jupiter), protection (Mars), wisdom (Mercury), and more.

R

Reality Manipulation

The practice of consciously shifting perception, probability, and physical circumstances in accordance with will. In high magik, this includes energy work, timeline shifting, and influencing synchronicities to shape reality.

Ritual Tool

Any physical object used in a magikal practice, such as an

athame (ritual blade), chalice, wand, or candle. These tools help to focus energy and act as conduits for spiritual forces.

S

Shielding

A defensive magikal practice that creates a protective energy barrier around oneself or a space. Shielding prevents unwanted spiritual influences, psychic attacks, and energy drains.

Sigil

A symbol charged with magikal intent, created by condensing a desire into a glyph. Sigils are activated through focused visualization, energy charging, or ritual use, making them powerful tools for manifestation.

Spirit Channeling

The act of allowing a spirit or entity to communicate through the magician. This can manifest as spoken words, written messages, or internal impressions during trance states.

T

Theta State

A deep meditative brainwave state (4–7 Hz) associated with trance, heightened intuition, and spiritual experiences. This state is ideal for astral travel, spirit communication, and deep magikal workings.

V

Visualization

A core technique in magik where the practitioner forms strong, clear mental images to direct energy and manifest results. Effective visualization enhances spellwork, pathworking, and sigil activation.

About The Author

Dave is an author of adult fantasy (The Furies series) as well as author of occult books about magick. Dave has multiple advanced degrees in the occult, including a Doctorate in Literature, plus Doctor Honoris causa in Ancient Religions, Doctor Honoris causa in Demonology, Doctor Honoris causa in Divinity, Doctor Honoris causa in Magik.

He began working ritual magik back in the 1970s. He took a brief break, then used the power of this magik to create a photography career which took him to Los Angeles and work as a photographer for multiple magazines.

Dave has studied magik in all forms, and in 2018, released a three-part magik instruction course in High Magik. Thousands of students have benefited from David's unique teaching style, making ceremonial magik accessible to everyone.

Dave also has a series on Grecian Magick, exploring the

aspects of ceremonial magick with the gods and goddesses of ancient Greece.

Magik Books by David Thompson
Available as EPUB, Paperback and Hardcover (*)

High Magick Series
- High Magick 101
- Daemons of High Magick
- Daemons and the Law of Attraction*
- Magick of Astaroth*
- Hidden in Plain Sight
- Lilith: Goddess of Darkness and Light*
- Daemons of Fortune*
- Asmodeus King of Daemons*
- Goddesses of High Magick
- Protection Magik
- The Diviner's Handbook
- The Magik of Lucifer*
- The Magik of Freya and Frigg
- The Magik of Sorath
- Goddesses of Vengeance
- Magik of Genius Spirits
- Power of Pathworking

Norse Magik
- Odin and Thor

Grecian Magick Series
- Magick of Apollo
- Magick of Hermes
- Magick of Aphrodite
- Magick of Fortuna*
- Greco-Roman Wealth Magick*
- Magick of the Sirens/Magick of the Muses
- Hermes and the Akashic Records

Magik for Everyone Series
- Candle Magik for Everyone
- Magik of Love & Lust
- Mind Magik: Zen and the art of Manifestation.

Fiction Novels by David Thompson

The Furies Series
- Angels of Vengeance
- Descent into Tartarus
- Furies: Beginnings
- Brianna: Making of a Fury

To connect with Dave, you can check his website at https://davepsychic.com

Social media links are at https://davepsychic.com/social-media-links/